Victorian LACE

TODAY

Jane Sowerby

PUBLISHER
Alexis Yiorgos Xenakis

CHIEF EXECUTIVE OFFICER
Benjamin Levisay

EDITOR
Elaine Rowley

DIRECTOR, PUBLISHING SERVICES
David Xenakis

TECHNICAL EDITOR
Lizbeth Upitis

TECHNICAL ILLUSTRATOR
Carol Skallerud

EDITORIAL COORDINATOR
Sue Kay Nelson

PRODUCTION DIRECTOR & COLOR SPECIALIST
Dennis Pearson

EDITORIAL ASSISTANT
Jennifer Dyke

BOOK PRODUCTION MANAGER
Greg Hoogeveen

GRAPHIC DESIGNER
Bob Natz

DIGITAL PREPRESS
Everett Baker
Nancy Holzer
Jay Reeve

PHOTOGRAPHER
Alexis Yiorgos Xenakis

PHOTO ASSISTANT
Mike Winkleman

MARKETING MANAGER
Lisa Mannes

PHOTO STYLIST
Rick Mondragon

BOOKS DISTRIBUTION
Karen Bright

MIS
Jason Bittner

SECOND PRINTING, 2006. FIRST PUBLISHED IN USA IN 2006 BY XRX, INC.

ISBN 1-933064-07-2
Produced in Sioux Falls, South Dakota, by XRX, Inc.,
PO Box 1525, Sioux Falls, SD 57101-1525 USA 605.338.2450

a publication of XRX BOOKS
visit us online - knittinguniverse.com

This book is dedicated
to the pioneering
Victorian women
who wrote the first
knitting books and
to the even more
adventurous women
who knit from them.

When I saw my first Shetland shawl, the softness, delicacy, and beauty of the lace patterns had me hooked. I knew I had to try lace knitting. One day, while wandering round an antique shop, I found a Victorian lace pattern in a dusty box of ephemera, and it began a new train of thought.

> Why had I not heard more about Victorian lace knitting?
> Why does Shetland dominate the scene today?
> When did Victorian knitting start, and what was the catalyst?
> Was it a leisure activity or did people sell this work?
> Who knitted—the wealthy with time on their hands, the
> poor out of necessity, or both?
> What yarns were available to the Victorians, and what colors would
> have been used at the time?
> How did knitting relate to their contemporary fashion, politics, and
> history?

I gradually built up a considerable collection of *Weldon's Practical Knitter* and other Victorian knitting and crochet publications, and it became apparent that to say there was a great deal of knitting in Victorian England was a massive understatement. Furthermore, much of it, especially towards the end of the century, was quite advanced—equal to the Shetland work, but of different style and construction.

One day, I found two books that made more sense of what I had found in Weldon's. Jane Gaugain's *The Lady's Assistant*, printed in 1840/41, and Miss Lambert's *My Knitting Book*, original printed in 1843, seemed to represent the origins of writing about hand knitting in England and Scotland. The works of these two ladies enabled me to see just how simple the beginnings of early written patterns were, and how rapidly hand knitting developed between 1840 and 1890.

Three other writers who made a significant contribution to knitting at this time were Miss Watts, Cornelia Mee (who produced many books over a thirty-year period, mainly on crochet), and Mlle. Riego de la Branchardière, who produced the *First Illustrated Knitting Book* in 1847, and won a Gold Medal for crochet at the Great Exhibition in 1851. In addition to those mentioned, numerous small publications abounded, often reminding the knitter how much her character would be improved by persevering in her art: busy hands kept a woman from idle or frivolous thoughts.

Unfortunately many of these old patterns, possibly from oral tradition, are muddled, inaccurate, and often in a style incomprehensible to the modern knitter. Some of the old knitting abbreviations need decoding. Weldon's in particular (especially the earlier editions) is full of inaccuracies and totally un-knittable patterns. I have spent many hours trying to make sense of these patterns by working them out on graph paper and making swatches. Sometimes I concluded that either they had never been knitted before printing, or that the printers had not checked the proofs.

This is such a vast subject that I have limited my explorations to lace knitting of shawls, scarves, etc. In order to answer my questions I had to investigate the beginnings of knitting which led to the epidemic of Victorian hand knitting; a little (but not too much) social and political history; Victorian fashion, especially the use of lace; dyes, colors, and yarns available in the nineteenth century; and the very earliest and simplest Victorian patterns; through to the stunningly advanced developments of the end of the century.

Foreword

This book traces the development of lace knitting in England through the work of a few pioneering ladies. Many more were involved in what became a huge industry, but I hope the works of the early knitters in their simplicity will inspire modern non-lace knitters to begin at the beginning and feel inspired to progress along with their Victorian predecessors.

If you are new to lace, I refer you to Understanding Lace and Charts on page 176, and especially the tips on page 177. Also, the project index on page 196 recommends several projects as first lace projects.

If you begin by choosing a yarn which really excites your imagination, either by its color(s) or by its feel, you are halfway to success. The next step is to find a shawl which is well within your capabilities. Don't worry if it is a very simple one—the yarn will transform it for you.

If you love the finished article, I suspect that you will be much more confident about knitting a slightly more demanding pattern second time around. I began this book as a knit/purl sweater knitter, with some trepidation, a lot of curiosity, and a determination to succeed. There were a lot of mistakes on the way, frustration at some of my early attempts at perfection, and an increasing joy and excitement as lace knitting became a real pleasure.

So please, don't hesitate to begin at the beginning, just as the Victorians did, and welcome to a wonderful knitting adventure.

Knitters new to lace
Look to Understanding Lace & Charts on page 176 before beginning. It will give you a good understanding of lace and its techniques before starting with one of the projects marked with an * in the project index on page 196.

THE LADY'S WORK BOOK.

XIV. — PYRENEES KNIT SCARF.

Foundation, six vandykes of blue; 24 rows of white, and 20 of blue alternately, the white and blue form a wave stripe; the stitch resembles rows of chain work. The Scarf is about two yards and a half long; finished by drawing up a both ends and attaching a tassel thereto. It requires 2½ oz. of each of the wools. Work with two pins of No. 9. Cast on, with blue Berlin wool, 125 loops.

1st Row	.	
2nd Row. P3 edge,	Plain	
3rd Row B3 edge	O, Tr, P15, T, O, P,	P2 edge.
4th Row P3 edge,	B O L B13 Lr O B2	
5th Row. B3 edge,	O, Ti, O, Tr, P11, T, O, T, O, P,	B2 edge
6th Row. P3 edge,	B, O, L, O, L, B9, Lr, O, Lr, O, B2,	P2 edge
7th Row. B3 edge,	O, Ti, O, Ti, O, Tr, P7, T, O, T, O, T, O, P,	B2 edge.
8th Row. P3 edge,	B, O, L, O, L, O, L, B5, Lr, O, Lr, O, Lr, O, B2,	P2 edge.
9th Row. B3 edge,	O, Ti, O, Ti, O, Ti, O, Tr, P3, T, O, T, O, T, O, T, O, P,	B2 edge.
10th Row. P3 edge,	B, O, L, O, L, O, L, O, L, B, Lr, O, Lr, O, Lr, O, Lr, O, B2,	P2 edge.
	O, Ti, O, Ti, O, Ti, O, Ti, O, Ar, O, T, O, T, O, T, O, T, T, P,	B2 edge.

* The edge stitches are never repeated; they are merely worked at the beginning and end of each row.

This finishes the vandyke; continue repeating the two last rows 24 times with blue, and 20 with white, till the scarf is the proper length; then knit as following receipt, beginning on a front row: —

11th Row. P3 edge,	P2, O, Ti, O, Ti, O, Ti, O, Ar, O, T, O, T, O, T, O, P3,	
12th Row. B3 edge,	B3, O, L, O, L, O, L, B, Lr, O, Lr, O, Lr, O, B4,	P2 edge.
13th Row. P3 edge,	P4, O, Ti, O, Ti, O, Ar, O, T, O, T, O, P5,	B2 edge.
14th Row. B3 edge,	B5, O, L, O, L, B, Lr, O, Lr, O, B6,	P2 edge.
15th Row. P3 edge,	P6, O, Ti, O, Ar, O, T, O, P7,	B2 edge.
16th Row. B3 edge,	B7, O, L, B, Lr, O, B8,	P2 edge.
17th Row. P3 edge,	P8, O, Ar, O, P9,	B2 edge.
18th Row. B3 edge,	Pearl row,	P2 edge.
19th Row,	Cast off.	B2 edge.

This scarf is very handsome when done with glover's silk.

Explanation of Terms. —O, make a stitch. —Tr, take in, reversed, by knitting two loops together from back part of loops, which throws the take-in stitch the reverse way of the plain take-in. —P15, fifteenth plain stitches. —T, take-in, by knitting two together. —P, a plain stitch. —B3, three back stitches. —B, a back stitch. —L, take in back stitch, by pearling two together. —Lr, take in back stitch revesred, by pearling first stitch, and slipping it on the left wire, then slip the next to it (on the left wire) over it; lift back the stitch that was pearled on to the right wire again. —Ti, take in, as described in index. —Ar, take in three, as per index.

A pattern from *The Ladies Knitting, Netting and Crochet Book* (known as *The Ladies Assistant*) by Jane Gaugain. As the first knitting author to use abbreviations, it appears she would have embraced today's charted patterns.

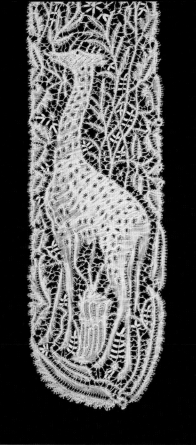

Knitting...

During the Victorian era everything and anything could be knitted, from fruit bowls to petticoats. Manuals contain patterns for every conceivable garment, from leggings (very practical in winter) to caps and bags. Antimacassars, tea cosies, cake covers, cushions and toys were all produced by the busy needles. Despite her apparent fragility, the Victorian woman clearly had a mania for productivity, and there was not a scrap of waste in the Victorian household.

The instructions for a *Knitted Moss Border*, 1886 demonstrate this all too clearly:
"This may be used for a variety of articles, border for toilet & lamp mats, cushions etc. The odds & ends of one's workbasket may be used up in this way for a pretty foot mat for placing before the bed. Knit any variety of pieces together & sew onto a foundation after steaming.

Cast on enough stitches for double the width required, say 20, and knit very tightly in plain knitting, row by row, until a sufficient length has been obtained. Cast off & place the strip on a sieve over a basin of boiling water & cover it over to keep in the steam. When it has absorbed the steam, & while wet, iron it with a hot iron, placing an old handkerchief over it to save discolouring the wool, cut the strip down the centre & ravel the wool on each side. The curling of the wool gives it a resemblance to moss which is very pretty!"
—Weldon's Practical Knitter, Thirty-Eight Useful Articles for Ladies & Gentlemen, 1886

Real lace from France or Belgium had been highly prized for centuries as a luxury item and an indication of wealth and status, so its transition into knitting was a logical progression. The mesh ground of lace work closely resembles faggoting stitch (yo, k2tog), which is the basis of lace knitting, and from here it is possible to trace the beginning of lace shawls. Unfortunately, due to the fact that knitted shawls were practical items and therefore literally worn to death, few examples from previous centuries survive.

in Victorian England

From the mid-eighteenth century onwards, the expansion of the factory system caused tremendous upheaval in the lives of the working classes. Large chunks of the population moved rapidly from rural to urban areas, cottage industries disappeared as mass-production took hold, and many had no choice but to seek work in the new mills and factories. Owners of mills and factories, along with traders and merchants, grew incredibly wealthy, especially considering their often-lowly roots, but there remained a chasm between the rich and poor.

Many industrialists came from Puritanical, Methodist, or Quaker backgrounds, all creeds emphasizing simplicity of lifestyle, diligence, toil, and fear of God. Many had only basic education, and held firm views about the respective places of women and men in society.

At this time a new middle class woman began to emerge. She almost never worked in paid employment, had at least a couple of servants (domestic labor was very cheap), and large amounts of time on her hands. Often the wife of a factory owner, trader, or merchant, she needed a productive, respectable hobby in order to clothe herself and the family, furnish the home, and engage in charity work.

Sewing and needlework were the ideal practical and quiet occupations for the new lady and suitable reading matter centred on fashion, needlework, and light fiction. Numerous periodicals began catering to this new market by answering questions on etiquette.

From 1836 several women began to write and import knitting patterns, and knitting for pleasure grew in popularity at an amazing rate. Queen Victoria herself was a knitter; Albert read to her whilst she spun yarn, and in her old age the Queen knitted and crocheted cot covers for her grandchildren. Royal and aristocratic patronage helped the publication and sale of the new knitting books as there was no history of written patterns—these had previously been handed down orally by the (illiterate) rural knitters.

Middle and upper class women began to knit, often for charitable purposes, such as for the poor or for soldiers during times of war. Patterns were published in women's magazines, and the new popular pastime provided a great deal of pleasure while posing no greater challenge than the choice of colors! By the end of the century, the most simple, basic designs had developed into works of art.

Queen Victoria was never a trendsetter in fashion, partly because she produced seven children in the first ten years of her marriage, but she did have a weakness for lace, and her wedding dress and veil were lavishly decorated with handmade Honiton (Devon) lace. She was keen to promote home industries, despite the temptation of exquisite expensive laces from France and Belgium .

As the new machine-made laces came available more women were able to add these hitherto expensive luxuries to their clothing, and entire dresses could now be made in lace. By mid-century it was everywhere, especially knitted lace. Expensive yarns such as silk were used for lace edgings knitted on ultra-fine needles, cotton yarns for trimming household furnishings and wool or Alpaca yarns for shawls, using larger needles.

The Queen's advice to her son was
Affect not the extreme mode—it is the index of a little mind—but let elegance and simplicity be ever the prominent character of your dress.

It is safe to say that the London Society ladies who devoured fine French lace and could not live without their dressmakers did not share this admirably restrained view. However the Queen's views were reinforced in etiquette books and lasted until the 1960's!

Shawls grew larger as the century progressed, mainly due to the ever-increasingly wide skirts, and in March 1881 *The Girls' Own Paper* addressed its readers
against the crinoline…It is the duty of us all as individuals to make a resolute stand, and prevent a foolish and atrociously ugly fashion from enslaving us again…happily for us of late we English women have become much emancipated from the control of French fashions, and we are not so much afraid of displaying a little individuality in our dress.

Shortly after this the crinoline did give way to simpler skirts which allowed women to lead a more active lifestyle, but shawls were still loved for their warmth, drape and elegance, and probably will continue to be loved, even though shapes, sizes, colors and yarns may alter with changing fashions.

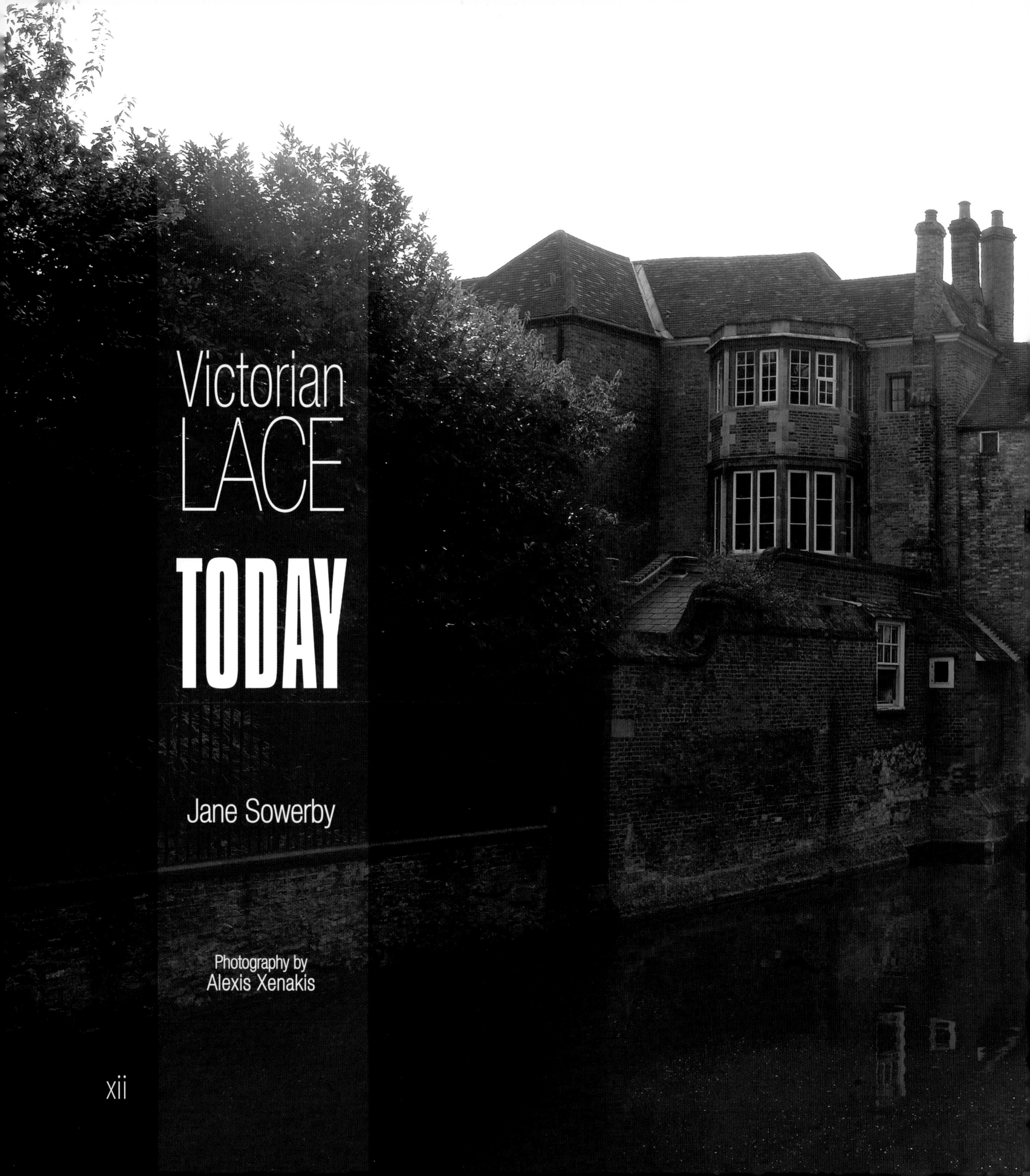

Victorian LACE TODAY

Jane Sowerby

Photography by
Alexis Xenakis

Table of Contents

Miss Watts and Mrs. Hope

A wide triangle   6

3

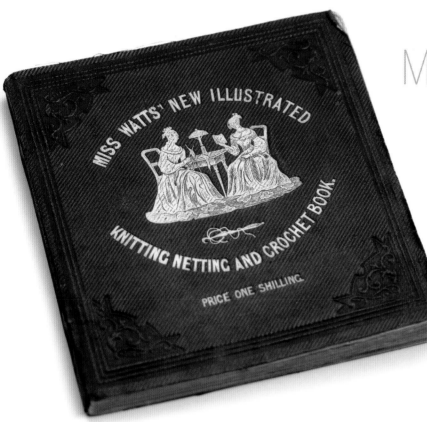

Miss Watts and Mrs. Hope

In 1837 *The Ladies' Knitting and Netting Book*, the first of its kind, appeared in London. It was "respectfully dedicated to Mrs. Annesley," but the compiler was Miss Watts who remained anonymous until 1842. It contained a very basic and practical set of patterns, and the modest list of patrons might have been family friends.

The earliest Vandyke edgings
Miss Watts' pattern for a Vandyke edging is the perfect place for an overview of Victorian lace knitting to begin. It forms the basis of all knitted lace edgings which were to develop as the century progressed. At this stage there were no holes or pattern motifs; just alternated plain and purled (stockinette and garter stitch) knitting in the shape of a pointed collar such as those worn in portraits by the seventeenth-century Flemish painter Sir Anthony Vandyke.

Miss Watts' edging, 1837
Cast on 2 sts and knit them.
Purl 1 row. Next row: Increase one stitch and knit the row. Continue this until there are 19 stitches. Next, rib 16, knit 3, and knit the next row. Continue until the piece is long enough and then decrease from a point.
Chart A shows my adaptation of this edging. The edging could be any size, or could begin with more stitches. In fact, it could go on forever.

Taking knitted edgings one stage further
Mrs. Hope, lace Vandyke edging for a cushion, 1847
This forms a useful lace for any purpose where a strong edging is required. Two knitting pins, No. 18, and rather coarse sewing cotton. Cast on eleven stitches, slip the first stitch, knit one, bring the cotton forward, knit two together, bring the cotton forward, knit two together, bring the cotton forward, knit two together, bring the cotton forward, and knit the rest plain; knit a plain row. Continue repeating these two rows until you get eighteen stitches on your pin. Then knit two rows plain. Next row, knit seven stitches plain, take two together, bring the cotton forward and take two together at the end of the row, knitting the last stitch plain. A plain row. Next row, knit six, take two together, bring the cotton forward, take two together, bring cotton &c., to the end of the row. A plain row; repeat the last two rows until you reduce the number on your pin to eleven stitches; begin again by knitting two rows plain. Always slip the first stitch. This pattern makes also a very pretty cuff.

In 1847, Mrs. Hope published *The Knitter's Friend*. It consisted of simple stitches such as Feather and Fan, and basic patterns for doilies, purses, and shawls, many of which appeared in Miss Watts' earlier book. Her Vandyke edging "for a cushion or a pretty cuff" is the template for a classic lace Vandyke with faggoting (yo-k2tog holes). It looks complicated but

Chart A, Miss Watts' edging

□ K on RS
▨ K on WS
○ Yo
⁄ K2tog

Repeat Rows 2 - 65
for edging.

Chart B, Mrs. Hope's Vandyke edging

CO 11

CO 2

is really only Miss Watts' edging partially filled in with faggoting. All the early authors gave variants of faggoting for a number of uses, including the center patterns of shawls, possibly because it was simple and quick to knit and emulated the ground of real lace, which was so fashionable at the time. I have used this for The Cap Shawl on page 26 and The Maltese Shawl on page 160.

The two edgings by Miss Watts and Mrs. Hope are given not just for the curiosity of the original instructions, but so that beginners to lace knitting can see how lace is constructed. More experienced lace knitters can use them as a basis for their own original borders (see page 165 Make Your Own Wide Border). Many of the later and more elaborate edgings consisted of either Miss Watts' basic edging with a motif inserted, or Mrs. Hope's version with width added by inserting more patterns (called insertions).

By referring to these edgings as Miss Watts' and Mrs. Hope's, I do not mean that the authors invented the edgings; rather that they passed the patterns down. The early knitting writers called their patterns *receipts*, which means literally that they were *received from someone*.

The language of knitting evolves
One problem with all the early knitting authors is that they left a great deal to the knitter. Explanations and instructions were sparse, to say the least. Even Mrs. Hope explains that her work
…was originally projected, not alone with a view to competition with other works of its kind, but from a belief that some improvements might be made, first in the descriptive phraseology, by avoiding at all times the use of two distinct terms to convey the same idea— a mode of expression which, however indifferent to those who, accustomed to knitting, have incidentally learned, that whether they 'purl,' 'rib,' 'seam,' or 'back stitch,' the action is the same, is enough to drive the novice nearly to despair; and secondly by entering more completely into details connected with making up the articles when knitted.

The cover of Mrs. Hope's book bears the words: "Patience, Perseverance, Application, Industry;" and the Victorian knitter certainly needed an abundance of all these attributes.

Miss Watts used different knitting terms from those of her contemporaries: *a turn* is two rows, *to narrow* is to "make small as if shaping a stocking" (we would *say decrease*), to *knit two into one* is to k2tog. To *take under* is to insert the needle purlwise, and *to increase or make a double stitch* is to knit twice into the same stitch. It is interesting to note that what we in England now call *plain knitting* (garter stitch in the U.S.) is referred to as *common knitting*.

An innovative pattern for a cape reads:
Knit a strip of double knitting two yards and a half long and about 40 stitches wide with coarse lambs wool on large needles. When you have finished this take finer needles and pick up all the stitches along one side, then continue with finest lambs wool putting the wool twice round the needle & 4 plain sts at each end for border. When ¾ yard deep, take even smaller needles & knit 1 row twice round (yo2) to run the ribbon in, then take up 3 stitches in every 1 stitch, and continue in plain knitting until the collar is long enough.

The use of finer needles and wool to provide automatic shaping was a real surprise. It also works very well with lace, especially since reducing stitch numbers in the middle of a pattern is to be avoided if at all possible.

Miss Watts' Spotted Shawl uses what must have been an old favorite stitch (yarnover, slip 1, knit 2, pass slipped stitch over) which reappeared throughout the century with different names (*open knit stitch*, Jane Gaugain; *shawl pattern*, Cornelia Mee; *star pattern*, Miss Lambert; *Dutch stitch*, Weldon's). We learn that " . . . a back row means a ribbed one." (*A purl row* in our terminology.) She took for granted the fact that her readers already had a basic understanding of knitting.

In 1845/6 The *Illustrated Knitting Netting and Crochet Book* appeared, price one shilling. This set of patterns included a knitted apron with a straight border in a simple leaf design—a classic Victorian favorite, a development of the old diamond pattern, and a palm pattern for a sofa guard. Miss Watts also includes a pattern for Gloucester boots, suggesting that they be soled by a shoemaker!

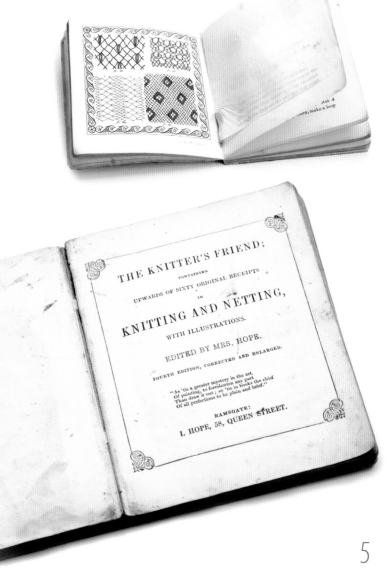

Miss Watts' edging can be any size, so I enlarged it until it became a triangular fichu—a shape that was fashionable around 1840. This wide, shallow triangle can be tied in a knot and worn at the shoulder, the hip, or any way you wish. A knit picot edging with a bead knitted onto every third picot adds a bit of weight and style.

A wide triangle
Using Miss Watts' knit edging

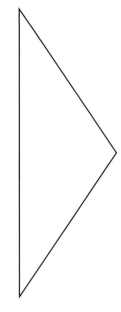

19" x 54"

10cm/4"

38

20

• over garter stitch
(knit all rows)

1 **2** 3 4 5 6

• *Fine weight*
265 yds

3.75mm/US 5, or size to obtain gauge

&

• stitch markers
• blunt needle
• 64 light-weight wooden beads
to fit yarn

HABU Tsumugi 1 cone
in 35 Whiskey

Notes
1 See *Techniques,* page 166, for yarn-overs. *2* It is essential to use light-weight beads.

Picot Cast on 2 stitches, bind off 2 stitches.

Picot with bead Cast on 2 stitches, place bead, bind off 2 stitches.

TRIANGLE
String beads onto yarn. Cast on 2 stitches.

Note The first half of the triangle is shaped by a yarn-over increase worked at the beginning of each wrong-side row.
Row 1 and all RS rows Knit.
Increase row 2 Picot with bead, yo, knit to end—1 stitch increased.
Increase row 4 Picot, yo, knit to end—1 stitch increased.
Increase row 6 Repeat Increase row 4.
Repeat Increase rows 2–7 thirty-two times (32 beads placed), or to center of triangle.

Note The stitch count remains the same over the next 6 rows. To maintain the yarn-over edge but not add a stitch, one decrease is worked after the yarn-over on each wrong-side row.
Center row 2 Picot with bead, yo, k2tog, knit to end.
Center rows 4, 6 Picot, yo, k2tog, knit to end.

Note The second half of the triangle is shaped by a pair of k2tog decreases. One decrease each wrong-side row maintains the count, and the second decrease shapes the shawl.
Decrease row 2 Picot with bead, yo, (k2tog) 2 times, knit to end—1 stitch decreased.
Decrease row 4 Picot, yo, (k2tog) 2 times, knit to end—1 stitch decreased.
Decrease row 6 Repeat Decrease row 4.
Repeat decrease rows 2–7 until 3 stitches remain.
Next WS row Picot with bead, yo, k3tog.
Bind off.

Block to measurements.

Decrease rows

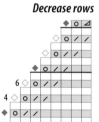

Continue as established until 32 beads placed + 5 rows = 193 rows. Work 6 center rows with no increase.

6 Center rows

| | | 6 | ◇ | o | / | | | | |

(chart)

☐	K on RS
▨	K on WS
o	Yo
/	K2tog
◿	K3tog
◇	Picot
◆	Picot with bead

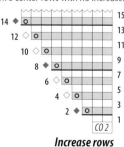

Increase rows

Mrs. Jane Gaugain

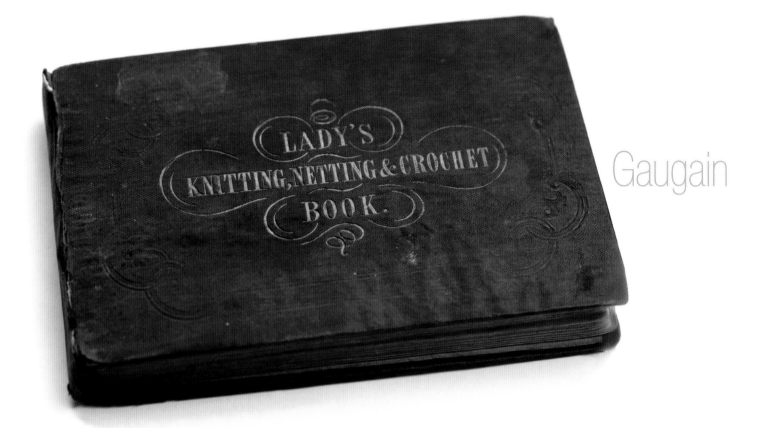

Gaugain

In submitting this Fourth and enlarged Edition of the following Work to the public, it affords me much pleasure in being able to state, that the flattering reception it has met with has exceeded my most sanguine expectations; and it is no slight gratification to me to find that my labours have been so highly appreciated, the result of the publication sufficiently indicating this. The method of explaining the receipts, though novel, and the only one occurring to me, has been found to answer the purpose completely, viz.that of giving a clear and simple explanation of them by means of letters and figures…
The Lady's Assistant—useful and fancy designs in knitting, netting and crochet, 1840/1, Preface to the fourth Edition

A total of sixteen books containing knitting patterns were published by Jane Gaugain between 1837 and 1854, and her final volume of *The Lady's Assistant*, for "…knitting shawls, scarfs [sic], edgings and fringes…" (the 22nd edition) was published in 1876, after her death: "…rearranged and improved by the Proprietor [I.J. Gaugain] … and sold by all Booksellers and Berlin warehouses."

In 1837, a year after printing what may well have been a trial run of her *Three Receipts for Friends*, Mrs. Gaugain produced her first *Small Work on Fancy Knitting*, and in 1840, *The Lady's Assistant* appeared, followed in 1846 by *The People's Book*. The latter, of which 23,000 copies were printed, appeared as a collection of "useful and saleable articles" for "females whose pecuniary means are limited, but whose minds and products are well regulated and directed," is evidence that ordinary people, as well as elderly ladies and the well-to-do, were beginning to knit for pleasure. In 1847 Jane

Gaugain's work had already reached the U.S.: a *Handbook of Needlework* was published in New York (now at Cornell University), and a supplement to this (now at Oberlin College, Ohio) under the joint authorship of Mrs. Jane Gaugain and Mrs. J.B. Gore.

The Pyrenees & Shetland Knit Shawl & Scarf Book was published in 1847, and for the first time one has a glimpse of what was to develop later on in the century. Real knitted lace, prettier designs and, though still practical, definitely not utilitarian articles in the strict sense. No doubt increased travel and Mrs. Gaugain's import business were partly responsible, but an evolution in lace knitting was beginning to take place. By 1854 Jane Gaugain had produced sixteen books of knitting patterns. She had made a very significant contribution to the beginning of Victorian knitting.

My copy of *The Lady's Assistant* was published in 1841. It was already in its fourth edition, and priced at five shillings and sixpence—quite an expensive knitting book at the time. The first edition was published in 1840, and since this copy is the fourth Edition, it would appear that Mrs. Gaugain's business and reputation were expanding rapidly. My copy is cloth-bound, measures 6½ x 4½ inches, and runs to 250 pages. The last four and a half pages contain an impressive list of patronesses and subscribers, (around 600) mainly Scottish ladies, listed in descending order of title, from Her Majesty the Queen Dowager, through Duchesses, Countesses, Viscountesses, and Rt. Hon. Ladies, to Mrs. and Miss. Her literary style is both practical and respectful, and I suspect that she was one of the upwardly mobile middle-class ladies of that time. By 1846 Volume 3 had appeared, and many ladies were clearly developing an interest in knitting.

Mrs. Gaugain's books do not reveal anything of a personal nature, but my daughter Helen discovered some fascinating evidence which gives added interest to her background. A certain John James Gaugain married Jane Alison (a common Scottish surname) on November 16, 1823, in the Parish of Edinburgh. They had three children. We do not know when Jane died, but her last book appeared posthumously in 1876, published "by the Proprietor" (of the warehouse).

The Scottish Trade Book Index lists "Gaugain, J(ohn) J(ames)" as "stationer and depot of materials for ladies' fancy works" at 63, North Bridge, Edinburgh, Scotland in 1823. Then, I.J. Gaugain, North Bridge 1824, 2 George St. 1825, "French blond and flower maker," 58 George St. 1826, "importer of French blond lace, manufacturer of flowers and braids" at the same address, 1827-8.

> Blondes were a type of light, airy lace that was all the rage from 1816. Light, lustrous lace, such as silk blondes, were popular as trimmings for dresses, the lace caps that were worn indoors, or hats and bonnets. They were usually ivory or cream, but could also be black, so *blonde* is not necessarily descriptive of color, but of lightness.
>> *"Blonde usually made [by the lacemakers] in the summer months [in France] in the open air, in winter in lofts over their cowhouses, warmed by the heat of their animals they dispensed with fire and its accompanying smoke."—History of Lace,* Mrs. Palliser, 1869

The Gaugains made further moves to 39, Frederick St. in 1827, 43 Frederick St. in 1832, and 63 George St. in 1837, where they stayed until 1852. Their six changes of address between 1823 and 1837 indicate an upwardly mobile family with increasing amounts of money. Also, according to the Scottish Trade Index, printed advertisements in The Edinburgh Directory of 1824 and 1835 show that Mr. Gaugain appears to have been a bookseller. His wife, Mrs. Jane Gaugain, ran the Berlin wool and other fancywork side of the business, and published a number of manuals on knitting and other craft work from 1840 onwards.

The most intriguing puzzle of all was the surname, Gaugain, seemingly French in origin. (Jane Gaugain was referred to as Madame Gaugain in an article on double knitting in *The Girls' Own Paper* of 1880). However, here is the story which we believe is probably true. In 1694 Thomas Gaugain came to England from France as a Huguenot (Protestant) refugee and was naturalized as an English citizen on 8th June 1694. He later became one of the Examiners of the Tellers Vouchers in the Exchequer—a Taxman!—and was probably the great grandfather of John James Gaugain who married Jane.

Now the Romantic story. It seems likely that there was a double wedding in Soho in 1787, for his grandsons Thomas and Peter married Marianne and Jane le Cointe. Jane Gaugain's husband was almost certainly the issue of one of these marriages. The le Cointes were also of Huguenot descent. Their family had been registered as Jewellers and Silk Merchants in Threadneedle Street—an area in which Huguenots had traditionally settled because of their trade—so the Gaugain's ownership of Warehouses selling lace, blondes, flowers, etc, would have been a natural progression. The term warehouse implied a rather more superior establishment than a shop and probably carried a much greater variety of stock.

In the preface to the fourth Edition, Jane Gaugain explains that she was the first person to invent "letters and figures–to give a clear and simple explanation of receipts," in other words, the first to use knitting abbreviations. She refers to stitches as *loops*, *B* back (purl), *P* plain (knit), *T* take in (knit two together), *F* yarn forward (and when inverted, yarn back), *A* SK2P (and when inverted, indicates SP2P), etc. These abbreviations are quite easy to learn, and the author was obviously proud of them, though other writers never used them. *Weldon's Practical Needlework* invented the system currently in use in 1906.

The patterns I have chosen from *The Lady's Assistant* represent some of the earliest examples of recreational knitting in 19th century Britain. Some are extremely simple, and consist of garter stitch and purl, eyelets and faggoting. Mrs. Gaugain generally used "knit two together" regardless of the direction of the stitches. If she did pay attention to the slant of increases and decreases she suggested some very cumbersome ways of producing SKP or SK2P.

> *Take in 3 loops into one (laying reversed to be taken in three) by knitting the first two off from the back part of the loops; slip it onto the left wire, lift it over the loop that was taken in then slip the take in loop onto the right wire again.*

The first two patterns that I have chosen to reproduce seem to be typical of the early lace patterns for amateur knitters—a sort of stage one on the progress chart. Some patterns were so simple that I almost dismissed them, until discovering that, with the right yarn and needles the result can be delightful. In order to bring these patterns into the 21st century I experimented with needle sizes and yarns, as the results obtained from original "receipts" must have been very close in texture—perhaps to keep out the cold. The answer for today's transformation seems to be using greatly increased needle sizes and a fine fluffy yarn such as a kid mohair blend.

One of the greatest delights of
Victorian shawls is the simplicity of their
construction. At first, they consisted of
garter stitch with fringed edging, or simple
yarn-over patterns known as faggoting.
Sometimes border patterns were added.
As the century progressed these borders
became wider and more elaborate, and the
faggoting began to form a frame between a
center pattern and the border.

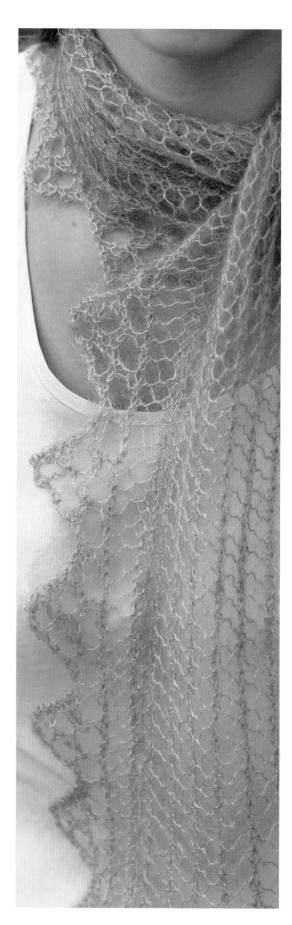

EASY LACE

20" x 58"

10cm/4"

26 / 18

• over stockinette stitch
(knit on RS, purl on WS)

1 **2** 3 4 5 6

• **Fine weight**
500 yds

4.5mm/US 7, or size to obtain
gauge, 60cm (24") or longer

Two 4mm/US 6

&

• stitch markers
• blunt needle
• small amount smooth yarn for
cast-on

ROWAN Kidsilk Haze
3 balls in 605 Smoke

Scarf or shawl
with a center pattern

Mrs. Gaugain gives several extremely simple patterns for shawls. This one is in faggoting—the basis of all lace knitting. The rectangle could be as big as you like—just cast on more stitches (after reading Note 2, below).

Corner A

Work 4 Single Joins (SJ), 1 Double Join (DJ)—1 repeat of Chart B.
Work 2 DJ on long side, 1 DJ on short side—1 repeat of Chart B.
Work 2 DJ, 2 SJ—1 repeat of Chart B.

Corner B

Work 2 SJ, 2 DJ—1 repeat of Chart B.
Work 1 DJ on short side, 2 DJ on long side—1 repeat of Chart B.
Work 1 DJ, 4 SJ—1 repeat of Chart B.

Notes

1 See Techniques, page 166, for lace cast-ons, yarn-overs, knitted-on border (including Single Join and Double Join), grafting, and blocking. *2* To lengthen (shorten), add (subtract) 6 repeats of Chart A for each Border repeat on long sides. To widen (or narrow), add (or subtract) two repeats of Chart A for each Border repeat on short sides.

CENTER PANEL

Note Slip first stitch of each row purlwise with yarn at wrong side (sl 1).
Using a lace cast-on, cast on 59 stitches (multiple of 3 + 2) onto circular needle. Knit 1 row. Purl 1 row.
Work 2-row repeat of Chart A, marking last stitch of Row 1 of seventh repeat and working chart a total of 132 repeats.
Next row Knit 2 together, knit to end of row—58 stitches. Purl 1 row. Leave stitches on circular needle. Cut yarn.

BORDER

Work knitted-on border Using a lace cast-on, cast on 7 stitches onto double-pointed needle (dpn). Beginning at marked slip stitch at left edge of center panel, * work 12-row repeat of Chart B 20 times, working 6 Single Joins for each repeat.
Continue working Chart B, joining border to center panel as follows: Work Corner A. [Work 6 Single Joins—1 repeat of Chart B] 8 times. Work Corner B. Repeat from *, placing 58 loops from cast-on edge onto circular needle before starting Corner A. Place loops from border cast-on edge onto free dpn. Cut yarn and graft ends together.

Block piece to measurements.

16

How to count 2-row repeats of faggoting

When knitting-on the border, it's important to have knit the correct number of repeats of the center pattern. With a repeat of only 2 rows, that will be a big number; but counting is easy with most lace patterns. As the chart shows, each 2-row repeat of Chart A contains 2 yarn-overs. Since they are offset, count the yarn-overs that align vertically to check the number of repeats you have knit.

Understanding lace

If you are new to lace knitting you could use this pattern as a starting point; it is repetitive and will enable you to observe the formation of the stitches. First knit a small swatch of the faggoting pattern (Chart A). On Row 2, notice that the purl-1 after purl-2-together is purled into the yarn-over of the previous row. Also, the first stitch of a knit-2-together or purl-2-together group is always a little looser than the one that follows, and it slants to the left. If you learn to recognize the stitches in this way, it will help with more difficult patterns which you will tackle later. Although lace looks complicated, it is really about being aware of the slant of stitches, (to the right or to the left), and the position of yarn-overs. If you understand the formation of a stitch pattern, you can recognize when it goes wrong and learn to put it right. The most common mistake is the omission of a yarn-over. If this occurs, pick up the thread between the two adjacent stitches to provide the missing stitch.

Chart A, Faggoting

Chart B, Border

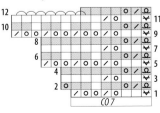

	K on RS, p on WS
	K on WS
O	Yo
/	K2tog on RS, p2tog on WS
/	K2tog on WS
V	Slip st purlwise with yarn at WS
⌄	Slip st purlwise with yarn at RS
℺	K border st tbl tog with 1 center panel st
⌒	Bind off 1 st

17

When young Queen Victoria ascended the throne in 1837, women began to follow her lead in dress and manner. The middle-class virtues of steady, God-fearing respectability that she embodied influenced fashion. Skirts lengthened, décolletage retreated, and feet disappeared under yards of petticoats and ever-wider skirts; women rapidly began to look very demure. By the 1830's, bonnet veils were one yard square and completely obscured the face, with a patterned border on three sides and a ribbon drawstring on the fourth. Not only did a shawl provide warmth, it was a modest cover-up for décolleté dresses. Mrs. Gaugain suggested that a shawl should be "for throwing over the shoulders indoors, or for very young ladies wearing out-of-doors."

It is interesting to compare this simple border with some of the wide and elaborate borders which appear towards the end of the century, and later in this book.

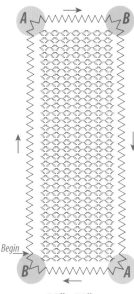

22" x 78"

10cm/4"
26
18
• over stockinette stitch (knit on RS, purl on WS)

1 **2** 3 4 5 6

• Fine weight
750 yds

4.5mm/US 7, or size to obtain gauge, 60cm (24") or longer

Two 4mm/US 6

&

• stitch markers
• blunt needle
• small amount smooth yarn for cast-on

ROWAN Kidsilk Haze
4 balls in 595 Liqueur

Large rectangle
with center diamond pattern

I have chosen the diamond pattern partly for its simplicity and partly because it is one of the earliest Victorian lace patterns.

Corner A
Work 4 Single Joins (SJ), 1 Double Join (DJ)—1 repeat of Chart B.
Work 2 DJ on long side, 1 DJ on short side—1 repeat of Chart B.
Work 1 DJ, 4 SJ—1 repeat of Chart B.

Corner B
Work 4 SJ, 1 DJ—1 repeat of Chart B.
Work 1 DJ on short side, 2 DJ on long side—1 repeat of Chart B.
Work 1 DJ, 4 SJ—1 repeat of Chart B.

Note
See *Techniques*, page 166, for lace cast-ons, yarn-overs, SSK, SK2P, knitted-on border (including Single Join and Double Join), grafting, and blocking.

CENTER PANEL
Note Slip first stitch of each row purlwise with yarn at wrong side (sl 1).
Using a lace cast-on, cast on 67 stitches (multiple of 9 + 4) onto circular needle.
Knit 1 row, purl 1 row.
Work 10-row repeat of Chart A, marking last stitch of Row 3 of second repeat and working chart a total of 36 repeats.
Next row Knit 2 together, knit to end of row—66 stitches. Purl 1 row. Leave stitches on circular needle. Cut yarn.

BORDER
Work knitted-on border Using a lace cast-on, cast on 7 stitches onto double-pointed needle (dpn).
Beginning at marked slip stitch at left edge of center panel, * work 12-row repeat of Chart B 28 times, working 6 Single Joins for each repeat.
Continue working Chart B, joining border to center panel as follows: Work Corner A. [Work 6 Single Joins—1 repeat of Chart B] 9 times. Work Corner B. Repeat from *, placing 66 loops from cast-on edge onto circular needle before starting Corner A.
Place loops from border cast-on edge onto free dpn. Cut yarn and graft ends together.

Block piece to measurements.

Chart A, Center Panel

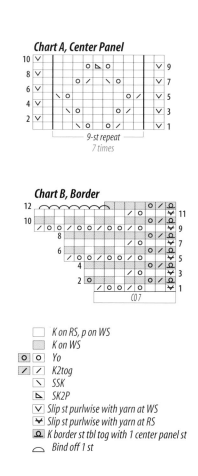

9-st repeat
7 times

Chart B, Border

C07

- ☐ K on RS, p on WS
- ▨ K on WS
- ⊙ Yo
- ⁄ K2tog
- ⟍ SSK
- ⟎ SK2P
- ⋁ Slip st purlwise with yarn at WS
- ⋎ Slip st purlwise with yarn at RS
- ⍟ K border st tbl tog with 1 center panel st
- ⌒ Bind off 1 st

Historic note

In the appendix at the end of *The Lady's Assistant,* there is a collection of stitches for various purposes. I have chosen what the author described as "a very pretty close diamond surrounded by open stitch" and "a knit edging for collarets, cuffs, petticoats & c." (I used the same edging to border the shawls on pages 14, 48, and 56.) In my copy, rows 7 and 8 have been added to this border pattern in ink by an unknown knitter, making the pattern twelve rows long instead of ten. I tried knitting both versions and preferred the longer one, not realizing that this was actually the same border as that given by Miss Lambert, Mrs. Gaugain's contemporary and possibly her rival. Could Mrs. Gaugain have borrowed Miss Lambert's pattern and deleted two rows to avoid plagiarism, or did Miss Lambert add two rows and a more upmarket title? We may never know, but competition was certain in the fast-moving world of knitting.

Understanding lace

The original diamond pattern only uses k2tog regardless of direction. Where appropriate, I have changed it to SSK. Since I find k3tog difficult to manage unless the tension is quite loose, I have also changed k3tog to SK2P. The original pattern suggested knitting the even-numbered rows (for garter-based lace), but I purled them (for stockinette-based lace).

Many of the early knitting books were divided into three sections: knitting, netting, and crochet. Netting appears to have been quite trendy as it resembled the ground of real lace and thus lightness, elegance, and luxury. Mrs. Gaugain's book contains three similar patterns: Spider Pattern, Spider Net, and A Kind of Spider Net. Spiders must have featured prominently among the list of residents in draughty Victorian houses!

Mrs. Gaugain's very pretty (and simple) shawl pattern appeared much later in Weldon's as a pattern for A Square Shawl with Spider Pattern Border and Insertion. Using Mrs. Gaugain's Spider Pattern with the later border (now knitted-on instead of sewn-on), I chose a rectangular shape for this new shawl.

Large rectangle
in spider net

INTERMEDIATE LACE

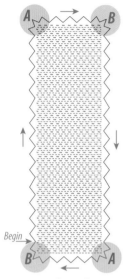

33" x 88"

10cm/4"

26 | 18

• over stockinette stitch
(knit on RS, purl on WS)

1 **2** 3 4 5 6

• Fine weight
1280 yds

4.5mm/US 7, or size to obtain
gauge, 60cm (24") or longer

Two 4 mm/US 6

&

• stitch markers
• blunt needle
• small amount smooth yarn for
cast-on

KNIT ONE, CROCHET TOO Douceur
et Soie 6 balls in 8248 Velvet Rose

24

Corner A

Work 2 Single Joins (SJ), 6 Double Joins (DJ), 4 Triple Joins (TJ) on long side (Rows 30 and 32 of first Border repeat plus Row 2 of next Border repeat form first TJ), 2 TJ on short side—2 repeats of Chart B.
Work 1 TJ, 3 DJ, 7 SJ—1 repeat of Chart B.

Corner B

Work 7 SJ, 3 DJ, 1 TJ—1 repeat of Chart B.
Work 2 TJ on short side, 4 TJ on long side (Row 32 of one border repeat plus Rows 2 and 4 of next repeat form last TJ), 6 DJ, 2 SJ—2 repeats of Chart B.

Note

See *Techniques*, page 166, for lace cast-ons, SSK, SKP, knitted-on border (including Single Join, Double Join, and Triple Join), grafting, and blocking.

CENTER PANEL

Note Slip first stitch of each row purlwise with yarn at wrong side (sl 1). Using a lace cast-on, cast on 75 stitches (multiple of 6 + 9) onto circular needle.

Next row (RS) K2tog, knit to end of row—74 stitches. Knit 3 rows. Work 8-row repeat of Chart A, marking last stitch of Row 5 of third repeat and working chart a total of 57 repeats. Knit 4 rows. Leave stitches on circular needle. Cut yarn.

BORDER

Work knitted-on border Using a lace cast-on, cast on 25 stitches onto double-pointed needle (dpn).
Beginning at marked slip stitch at left edge of center panel, * work 32-row repeat of Chart B 13 times, working 16 SJ for each repeat.
Continue working Chart B, joining border to center panel as follows: Work Corner A. [Work 16 SJ—1 repeat of Chart B] 3 times. Work Corner B. Repeat from *, placing 74 loops from cast-on edge onto circular needle before starting Corner A.
Place loops from border cast-on edge on free dpn. Cut yarn and graft ends together.

Block piece to measurements.

Chart A, Shawl

6-st repeat
11 times

☐ K on RS, p on WS
▨ K on WS
⊙ Yo
╱ K2tog on RS, p2tog on WS
╱ K2tog; or SSK for directional decrease
╲ SSK
╱ P2tog on RS
◣ SK2P
∨ ∨ Slip st purlwise with yarn at WS
¥ Slip st purlwise with yarn at RS
Ω K border st tbl tog with 1 center panel st

Chart B, Wide border in spider pattern

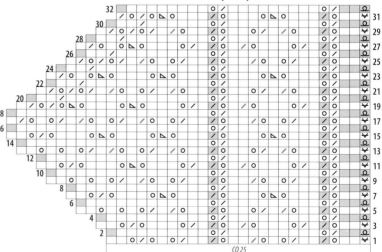

CO 25

Historic note

This shawl uses a wide border and insertion in the same stitch from around the time of Queen Victoria's death; for an optional narrow border see number 13 from *The Lady's Assistant for shawls, scarfs, edgings and fringes* by Jane Gaugain (1876; published posthumously), on page 183.

Understanding lace

Notice that despite the apparent intricacy of the wide border there are still no directional decreases. Also, see how faggoting both extends the pattern and divides it for clarity. Red symbols on the chart indicate decreases to change for directional decreases, if you prefer.

In *The Lady's Assistant*, there is a pattern for a baby's knit cap, described as "very beautiful." A circle forms the crown of the cap as a nine-pointed star, and the garment was originally worked with very fine cotton and No. 23 pins (approximately 0.559mm). When knit with larger yarn and needles, it makes the perfect center for a circular shawl.

The cap shawl

INTERMEDIATE LACE

74" diameter

10cm/4"

26

18

• over stockinette stitch
(knit on RS, purl on WS)

1 **2** 3 4 5 6

• *Fine weight*
1700 yds

4.5mm/US 7, or size to obtain
gauge, 40–100cm (16–40") long
as stitch number increases

4.5mm/US 7

&

• stitch markers
• blunt needle

ROWAN Kidsilk Haze
8 balls in 606 Candy Girl

This shawl began as a pattern for the crown of a baby's cap by Mrs. Gaugain (1840), was extended to a shawl by *Weldon's* (1886), and is now reproduced with a similar (not identical) border by Mrs. Hope (1847).

Notes
1 See *Techniques*, page 166, for circle cast-on, lace cast-ons, knitted-on border (including Single Join), grafting, and blocking. *2* Begin with double-pointed needles (dpn); change to 16" circular, then to longer circulars as number of stitches increases. *3* Place markers between each section of shawl.

SHAWL
Using circle cast-on, cast on 9 stitches (1 for each section of shawl) onto 3 double-pointed needles (dpn). Join and begin working in rounds.

Work Chart A, Rounds 1–38—180 stitches.

Rounds 39–84 Work as established, working an additional eyelet (yo, k2tog) every 4 rounds—387 stitches.

Work Chart B, Rounds 85–172—738 stitches. Leave stitches on circular needle. Cut yarn.

BORDER
Work knitted-on border Using a lace cast-on, cast on 11 stitches onto dpn. Work 30-row repeat of Chart C, working 15 Single Joins for each repeat EXCEPT at 3 points distributed around shawl, attach border to 2 shawl stitches. When you reach the point on the shawl where the border began, pick up stitches from border cast-on edge on free dpn. Cut yarn and graft ends together.

Block piece to measurements.

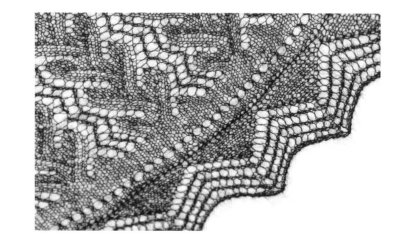

Chart A, Shawl

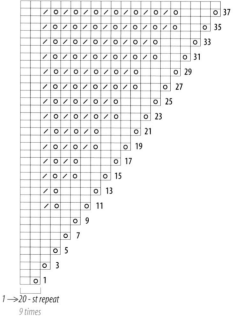

Chart A (rows read right to left, odd rows numbered):

- Row 37: / o / o / o / o / o / o ... o
- Row 35: / o / o / o / o / o / o ... o
- Row 33: / o / o / o / o / o / o o
- Row 31: / o / o / o / o / o o
- Row 29: / o / o / o / o / o o
- Row 27: / o / o / o / o / o o
- Row 25: / o / o / o / o o
- Row 23: / o / o / o / o o
- Row 21: / o / o / o o
- Row 19: / o / o / o o
- Row 17: / o / o / o o
- Row 15: / o / o o
- Row 13: / o o
- Row 11: / o o
- Row 9: o o
- Row 7: o o
- Row 5: o o
- Row 3: o o
- Row 1: o

1 → 20 - st repeat
9 times

Chart B

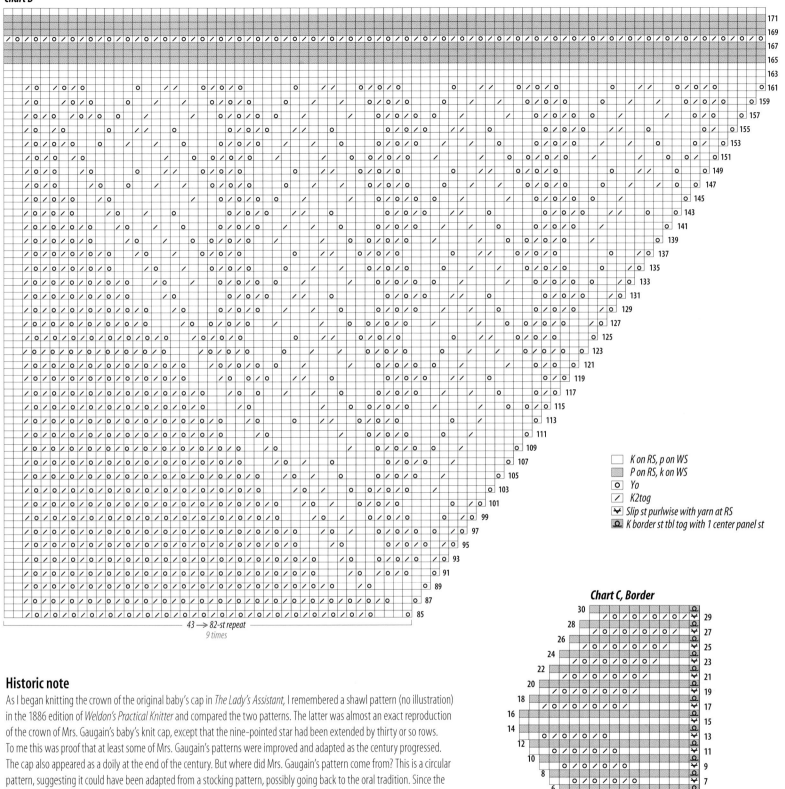

43 → 82-st repeat
9 times

Legend:
- ☐ K on RS, p on WS
- ▨ P on RS, k on WS
- ⊙ Yo
- ∕ K2tog
- ☒ Slip st purlwise with yarn at RS
- ☒ K border st tbl tog with 1 center panel st

Chart C, Border

CO 11

Historic note

As I began knitting the crown of the original baby's cap in *The Lady's Assistant*, I remembered a shawl pattern (no illustration) in the 1886 edition of *Weldon's Practical Knitter* and compared the two patterns. The latter was almost an exact reproduction of the crown of Mrs. Gaugain's baby's knit cap, except that the nine-pointed star had been extended by thirty or so rows. To me this was proof that at least some of Mrs. Gaugain's patterns were improved and adapted as the century progressed. The cap also appeared as a doily at the end of the century. But where did Mrs. Gaugain's pattern come from? This is a circular pattern, suggesting it could have been adapted from a stocking pattern, possibly going back to the oral tradition. Since the Weldon's version of the cap shawl was knit on double-pointed needles, I suspect that few knitters would have attempted it, despite being familiar with stocking knitting.

"At the request of many ladies, who were doubtful of succeeding in forming a shawl from the cushion receipt in the accompaniment to the Second Volume of my work, I have been induced again to present that beautiful specimen of knitting, extended for the above purpose. It can be worked all white; or white centre and coloured shaded border; say twelve shades of gold colour, commencing at the lightest . . . .
To a person of taste, there is great scope for variety . . . . The beauty of this is the simplicity—alternating stripes of graduated colour and white—seven shades of pink embroidery wool . . . ."

— Jane Gaugain

A handsome triangle

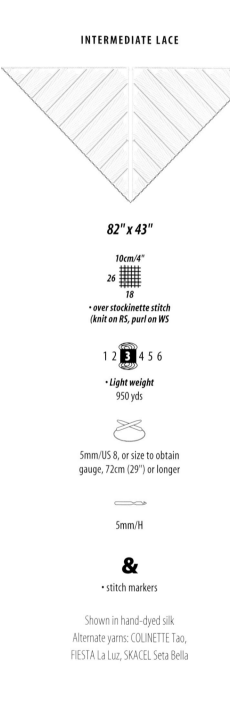

INTERMEDIATE LACE

82" x 43"

10cm/4"
26 ▦
18
• over stockinette stitch
(knit on RS, purl on WS

1 2 **3** 4 5 6
• *Light weight*
950 yds

5mm/US 8, or size to obtain
gauge, 72cm (29") or longer

5mm/H

&
• stitch markers

Shown in hand-dyed silk
Alternate yarns: COLINETTE Tao,
FIESTA La Luz, SKACEL Seta Bella

Notes

1 See *Techniques,* page 166, for crochet bind-off and blocking. *2* Place markers at beginning and end of pattern repeats and at center of shawl.

SHAWL

Cast on 4 stitches: 2 for each half of the shawl.

Work Chart A, Rows 1–120.

* ***Rows 121–166*** Work as Rows 29–74 EXCEPT there are five 20-stitch repeats of the lace pattern.

Rows 167–212 Work as Rows 75–120 EXCEPT there are seven 20-stitch repeats of the lace pattern.

Note To make a larger shawl or to use a finer yarn, continue to alternate Rows 75–120 with Rows 29–74, working each 46-row repeat with two more 20-stitch repeats of the lace pattern.

Do not cut yarn.

Bind off with a crochet hook: * Chain (ch) 8, single crochet (sc) in next shawl stitch, ch 4, sc in next stitch; repeat from *.

Block piece to measurements.

Chart A

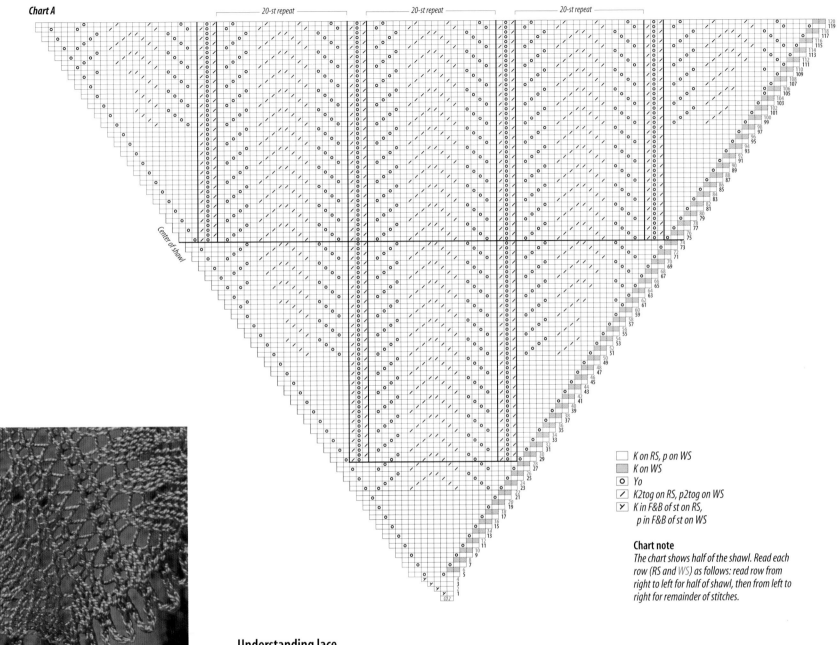

	K on RS, p on WS
▨	K on WS
◉	Yo
╱	K2tog on RS, p2tog on WS
⅄	K in F&B of st on RS, p in F&B of st on WS

Chart note
The chart shows half of the shawl. Read each row (RS and WS) as follows: read row from right to left for half of shawl, then from left to right for remainder of stitches.

Understanding lace

The shawl begins with one pattern repeat at each side of the center of the hypotenuse. As stitches are gradually increased, new pattern repeats are formed. The triangle grows in this way and can be any size you wish. Just carry on knitting until you run out of yarn! Once the 4-row sequence is understood, it is quite fun to knit. When the shawl is large enough, finish with a crochet bind-off, with Mrs. Gaugain's knitted border (page 21), or Bell ruffle (page 179). Do not bind off in the normal way or the edge will be too tight.

Historic note

Mrs. Gaugain says: "Some ladies may think it immaterial whether they work backwards from the centre, or repeat again from the beginning of the row, but it is most material to work as I have described in this row, as the end and beginning of many rows are different, consequently, if repeated again from the beginning of the row, it would make the pattern wrong."

This scarf pattern, dated 1847, was one of the most delightful surprises I encountered in my voyage of discovery. Most patterns from this period are far less elaborate. While extra concentration is required in knitting this piece initially, it is not difficult once the layout is understood. This fascinating border is true knitted lace, as every row of the repeat is patterned.

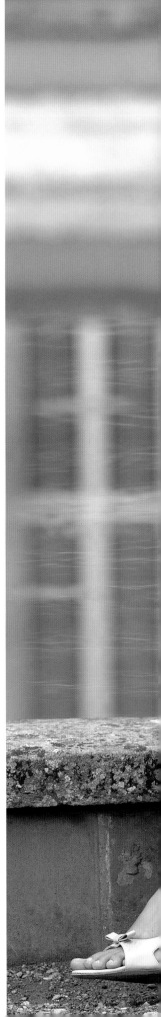

Alpine knit scarf
with double rose leaf center pattern and diamond border

18" x 65"

10cm/4"

28
22

• over stockinette stitch
(knit on RS, purl on WS)

1 2 3 4 5 6

• **Super Fine weight**
850 yds

Straight or circular
3.5mm/US 4, or size
to obtain gauge

&

• stitch markers
• blunt needle

Shown in PATON'S Baby Merino
2-ply wool, white
Alternate yarn: LORNA'S LACES
Helen's Lace

"This very beautiful and light Scarf is composed of a border of diamonds all round; and the center is stripes of the double rose leaf."—Jane Gaugain

Note
See *Techniques*, page 166, for p2tog, SSK, SK2P, k3tog, suspended bind-off, and blocking.

SHAWL
Loosely cast on 121 stitches (multiple of 18 + 13). **Next 8 rows** Slip 1 purlwise with yarn at wrong side (sl 1), knit to end of row.
Lower border
Work 16-row repeat of Chart A 3 times.

Transition
Establish right and left borders and garter-stitch center,
Next row (Row 1 of Chart A) Work first 25 stitches of chart, ending k2tog instead of SK2P (right border, place marker); knit 71 (place marker); work last 25 stitches of chart, beginning k2tog instead of SK2P (left border).
Next 6 rows Work right and left border as established, and knit 71 center stitches for 4 ridges of garter stitch.
Next row Work as established, EXCEPT increase 7 stitches evenly spaced across garter-stitch center—128 stitches, 78 center stitches.

Center section
Continue right and left borders with rose leaf center, Next row
Work Row 9 of Chart A for right border; work Row 1 of Chart B across center stitches as follows: work first 5 stitches, place marker, work four 17>15-stitch repeats, placing marker after each, work last 5 stitches; work Row 9 of Chart A for left border—120 stitches, 70 center stitches. Continue working in patterns as established for thirty-seven 8-row repeats of Chart B; because the diamond repeat is 16 rows and the double rose leaf-repeat is 8 rows, the latter is knit twice for every 16-row repeat of diamonds. **Note** The stitch count in each rose-leaf repeat decreases from 17 to 15 stitches in Row 1 and increases again to 17 in Row 7—128 >120>128 stitches, 78>70>78 center stitches.

Transition
Next row Continue borders; knit center stitches, decreasing 7 stitches evenly across (k2tog)—121 stitches.
Next 7 rows Work borders and 71-stitch garter-stitch center.

Top border
Work three 16-row repeats of Chart A, as at beginning of shawl.
Next 8 rows Sl 1, knit to end of row.
Bind off loosely using suspended bind-off.

Block piece to measurements. On both ends, pin only the points of diamonds to form scallops.

Chart A, Diamond border

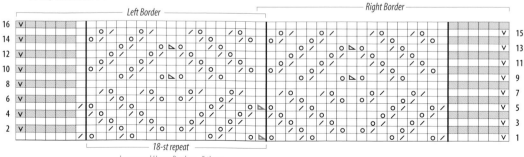

Lower and Upper Borders - 5 times

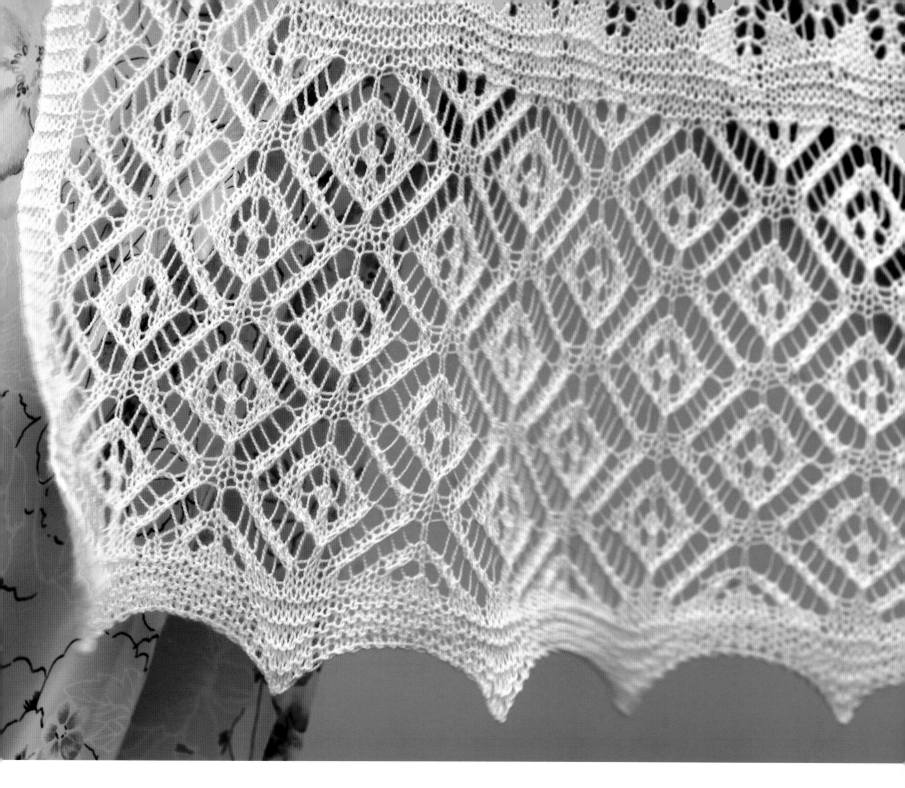

Chart B, Rose leaf center pattern

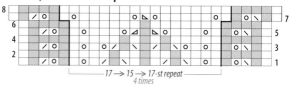

17 → 15 → 17-st repeat
4 times

- ☐ K on RS, p on WS
- ▨ P on RS, k on WS
- ⊙ Yo
- ╱ K2tog on RS, p2tog on WS
- ╲ SSK
- ◣ SK2P
- ◢ K3tog
- V Slip st purlwise with yarn at WS
- ◣ SK2P for lower and upper borders, K2tog for right and left borders

Historic note

The border appeared as "an open diamond (lace) pattern for stockings, shawls, etc." in Mrs. Gaugain's book of 1840/1. She advises, "before working the plain part [transition] pick up a stitch from the row below as you require it when the centre pattern begins," with no mention of how many stitches were needed! The double rose leaf appears to be a development of the single leaf pattern of the same time.

Miss Lambert

39

Miss Lambert

"The examples of knitting contained
in the following pages have been selected
with the greatest care–many are original–and the whole
are so arranged as to render them comprehensible to a novice in the
art. Knitting being so often sought as an evening amusement, both by
the aged and by invalids, a large and distinct type has been adopted, as
affording an additional facility."
—Miss Frances Lambert, *My Knitting Book*   1845/6

The second important author of knitting books was Miss Frances Lambert, who first published her *Handbook of Needlework* in 1842. *My Knitting Book* first appeared in 1843, but the copy used in my research (one of 32,000) is listed as the first series, with a publication date of 1846 by John Murray of Albermarle Street, London, price one shilling and six pence. It is probable that this is the one described in the preface as "having undergone a thorough revision in order to rectify inaccuracies."

Miss Lambert's *Handbook of Needlework* was also published in New York by Wiley and Putnam in 1842, and is "the earliest American pattern book" in the collection of *http://www.librarycompany.org*. The library catalogue describes "The English woman Frances Lambert" as "the most popular Needlework writer in 19th century America". She also wrote *The Ladies' Complete Guide to Needlework and Embroidery, My Crochet Sampler, Instructions for making Miss. Lambert's Registered Crochet Flowers, Practical*

Hints on Decorative Needlework, and *Church Needlework With Practical Remarks on its Arrangement and Preparation*. She was not only very knowledgeable and "a Lady of her time", but quite an astute businesswoman. At the beginning of her *Handbook of Needlework* she acknowledges the help and encouragement of her husband in the production of that work, so we know that she was, in fact, a married woman who preferred to retain a certain amount of anonymity.

Miss Lambert described herself as "Embroideress to the Queen", though according to The Royal Archives, G. Dalmaine and N. Lewis were the holders of that office from 1837–1851. However, on 22nd November 1837, Miss Lambert was given a warrant as "embroiderer in general" and "needlework woman in ordinary" to Her Majesty. This indicates that she was neither the only, nor the most senior embroideress to the Queen, but the title was no doubt a great help to her books and trade in fancy goods, just as royal warrants are in England today. Miss Lambert had already written several up-market books on embroidery by the time Jane Gaugain's first books appeared. With her royal connections and seemingly greater reputation, she writes confidently, and the materials she recommends are fine cottons, silk, and Berlin wool—expensive, imported yarns, suitable for upper-class women, or even royalty.

Comparing Miss Lambert and Jane Gaugain

The numerous piracies committed on her [Miss Lambert's] Handbook of Needlework, mainly led to the publication of this little treatise; yet, in more than one instance, the Authoress has been again compelled to claim, and successfully, the protection of the law against similar attempts to invade her copyright of the present volume, as also that of My Crochet Sampler.

Miss Lambert's suggestion that other writers were pirating her designs may have been partly true, but it is more likely that the patterns were circulating widely via the oral tradition. Miss Lambert complains of piracy, while Mrs. Gaugain's pattern for knitted edging is identical to Miss Lambert's Vandyke border, except the latter has two extra rows in the middle. Who is copying whom? However, Miss Lambert's Star pattern Shawl, her Vandyke Pattern and her Russian Shawl in Brioche Stitch closely resemble similarly named patterns in Jane Gaugain's book, so one might reasonably suppose that either both ladies were drawing from the same sources of material or that they themselves were guilty of piracy!

Without alluding to numerous petty piracies, the writer cannot refrain from noticing the reprint of this treatise in America dedicated to the ladies of the United States–a circumstance which she is fain to accept as a compliment, as there is no redress for the substantial wrong. To imitators at home, it may be as well to hint that all the designs in this volume are copyright.
—Advertisement to *Handbook of Needlework*, Second Edition, February, 1843

Both ladies were guilty of gross inaccuracies in their patterns, though it could have been the printer's fault. However, in stating "This Edition has again undergone a thorough revision . . . ," Miss Lambert does comment on " . . . how difficult it is to be accurate in a work of this kind . . .". Perhaps it was especially difficult to write down details of patterns previously handed down in the oral tradition. And a possible lack of mathematical education could have made the logical side of pattern planning difficult. There was no chart paper in those days, so I can visualize puzzled knitters getting together to gossip and try to sort out some of the nonsense in these patterns.

Miss Lambert has a much more confident style of writing than Mrs. Gaugain, possibly because she came from a slightly higher level of society. Certainly the colors she suggests in her knitting patterns are subtler than those in *The Lady's Assistant*. The address given at this time was 3, New Burlington St., off Regent St. in London, but I have found no trace of its use as a residence at this time. It was most likely a shared workshop/fitting room for seamstresses in quite an expensive area.

Unlike Jane Gaugain, Miss Lambert does not use a system of knitting abbreviations, but explains the terms used in knitting. Sometimes, economy of language would be something of a relief; here she describes how to knit and purl alternately in the same row:

"When the stitch next after a purl stitch, is to be knitted, it is obvious that the thread must be passed back UNDER the needle, before this can be done;—in like manner, when a stitch is to be purled, after a knitted one, the thread must be brought in front UNDER the needle:—processes, however, very different from those of passing the thread over, and bringing the thread forward, both of which are for the purpose of MAKING a stitch, and are done ABOVE the needle."

To complete the section on terms used in knitting, Miss Lambert states that the sizes of the needles are given according to her Standard Filière. This represented a real breakthrough into knitting as we know it today, for patterns could now be reproduced with confidence—or at least more confidence.

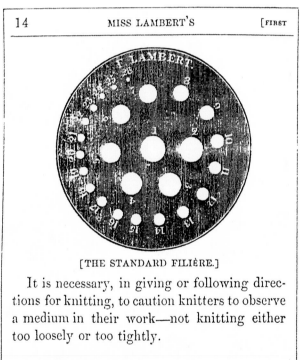

14   MISS LAMBERT'S   [FIRST

[THE STANDARD FILIÈRE.]

It is necessary, in giving or following directions for knitting, to caution knitters to observe a medium in their work—not knitting either too loosely or too tightly.

Siberian Cuffs.

Nine shades of German wool, used double, will be required.—Needles, No. 8.

These shawls can be knitted as either a hexagon (six sides), or as a half-hexagon. Miss Lambert's Barège pattern is such fun to knit that I had to find a stunning way of displaying it.

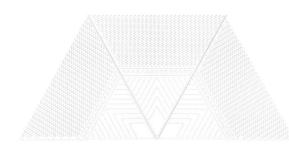

Half hexagon 84" x 36"
Full hexagon 72"
Fichu (half hexagon, center only)
42" x 20"

10cm/4"

26 **18**

• over stockinette stitch
(knit on RS, purl on WS)
using 4.5mm/US 7 needle

1 **2** 3 4 5 6

• Fine weight
Half hexagon 900 yds
Full hexagon 1800 yds
Fichu 600 yds

4.5mm/US 7, 5mm/US 8, 5.5mm/
US 9, and 6mm/US 10, or size to
obtain gauge, 60cm (24") or longer

Four (two), 4.5mm/US 7

5.5mm/I

&

• stitch markers
• For fichu: 79 glass beads to fit yarn

Shown in handspun Polworth/Kid
ROWAN Kidsilk haze
8 balls in 595 Liqueur
JAEGER Alpaca 4-ply
3 balls in 395 Damson
Alternate yarns: JADE SAPPHIRE
Cashmere 2-ply
or
TWISTED SISTERS Petite Voodoo

Spider's-web shawls

Notes
1 See *Techniques*, page 166, for crochet cast-on, circle cast-on, SSK, SK2P, S2KP2, knitted-on border, and blocking. *2* Mark stitch that divides sections (pink stitch on chart).

HALF HEXAGON
Notes 1 Begin and end each row of shawl with 2 garter stitches–not included in charts or stitch counts. *2* After Row 3, stitch counts are for only one section of shawl. Each section increases 2 stitches in odd rows.
Using 4.5mm/US 7, 24" circular needle, cast on 6 stitches (2 border stitches, 2 divider stitches, 2 border stitches).
Row 1 K2, [yo, knit dividing stitch] 2 times, yo, k2—9 stitches total, 1 stitch per section.
Row 2 and all even rows K2, purl until 2 stitches remain, k2.
Row 3 K2, [yo, k1, yo, knit dividing stitch] 2 times, ending yo, k1, yo, k2—15 stitches total, 3 stitches each section. Continue to work Chart A as established for Rows 4–68—67 stitches.
Rows 69–84 Work 16-row repeat, working each 8-stitch repeat 2 times—83 stitches.
Rows 85–100 Work 16-row repeat, working each 8-stitch repeat 3 times—99 stitches.
Change to 5mm/US 8 needle and work Chart B, Rows 101–117—117 stitches.
Next row (WS) K2, purl to last 2 stitches, increasing 1 stitch at beginning of each section, k2—118 stitches each section. Change to 5.5mm/US 9 needle and work Chart C, Rows 1–14—132 stitches.
Note Every 12-row repeat for each section begins and ends the same; the only difference is the number of 6-stitch repeats. Every 12 rows, 12 stitches are increased, adding 2 additional repeats.
Change to 6mm/US 10 needle and work 4 more 12-row repeats—180 stitches.
Bind off with crochet hook: * chain (ch) 8, single crochet (sc) in next shawl stitch, ch 4, sc in next stitch; repeat from *.

Block piece to measurements.

FULL HEXAGON
Note Begin with double-pointed needles (dpn); change to 16" circular, then to longer circulars as number of stitches increases. Circle cast-on 6 stitches onto dpn (1 for each section; 2 on each of 3 needles). Join and begin working in rounds.
Work chart patterns as follows [Work row of chart to next marker] 6 times.
Work chart-row sequence as for half hexagon through Chart B, Row 117, changing needle sizes as indicated.
Next round Knit, increasing 1 stitch at beginning of each section—118 stitches each section.
Work chart-row sequence as for half hexagon beginning with Chart C. Bind off with crochet hook as for half hexagon.
Block piece to measurements.

FICHU
Work as half hexagon through Row 100.
Note Following instructions and stitch counts are for entire fichu, including 4 garter-stitch edge stitches.
Next row (RS) K2, * (yo, k1) 2 times, (yo, k2tog) 48 times, yo, k1, yo, knit marked stitch. Repeat from * 2 more times, ending yo, k2—314 stitches.
Next row Knit.
Leave stitches on circular needle. Cut yarn. Work border.

BORDER
Note String beads onto yarn before beginning border.
Work knitted-on border Slip first stitch from needle onto crochet hook and crochet cast-on 7 stitches. Work 4-row repeat of Chart D as knitted-on border AND add a bead to outside edge every other Row 4: cast on 2 stitches, pull up bead, bind off 4 stitches, k3, yo, k2tog, k1.
Block piece to measurements.

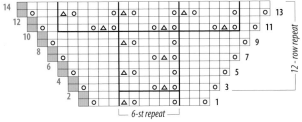

Chart A, Center

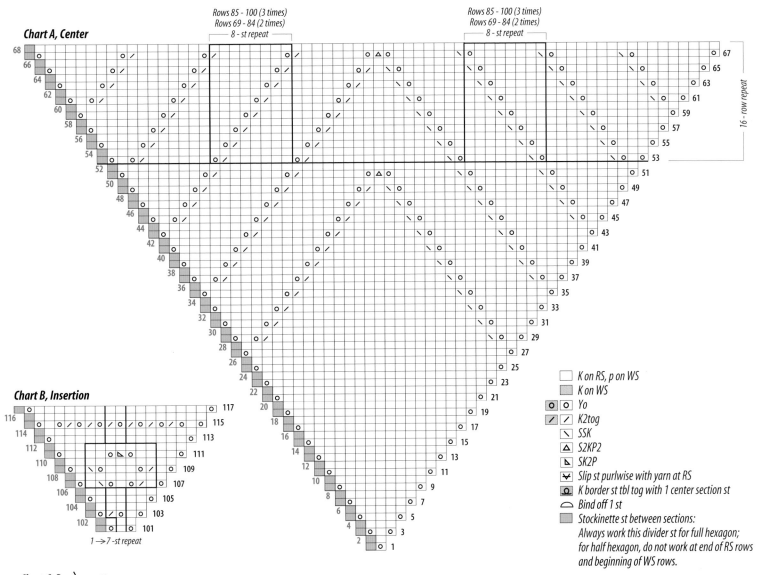

Rows 85 - 100 (3 times)
Rows 69 - 84 (2 times)
8 - st repeat

16 - row repeat

Chart B, Insertion

1 →7 -st repeat

Chart C, Barège pattern

12 - row repeat

6-st repeat

Chart D, Border 14

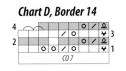

C0 7

	K on RS, p on WS
	K on WS
o o	Yo
/ /	K2tog
\	SSK
△	S2KP2
◣	SK2P
⊻	Slip st purlwise with yarn at RS
⍜	K border st tbl tog with 1 center section st
⌒	Bind off 1 st
	Stockinette st between sections: Always work this divider st for full hexagon; for half hexagon, do not work at end of RS rows and beginning of WS rows.

Historic note

Victorian houses were undoubtedly full of spiders, and unlike today, people probably saw them as a help to reducing the fly population. The concept of a spider's web shawl evolved from a pattern around the end of the century, but I did not find the original design particularly attractive, partly because it began as a hexagon and ended as a circle. Although the full hexagon would probably not have been knitted in 1846, the half hexagon would have been possible on long needles.

The principle of ray shaping was used to shape the nine-pointed star in Jane Gaugain's pattern for a baby's cap (page 26).

French printed Barège shawls (two yards square and named after a village in the Pyrenees) were very popular. It is possible that Miss Lambert's Barège pattern had come from France but just as likely that she was trying to emulate a current fashion as knitting.

Shetland shawls became popular in England after 1840 (the sea route to Shetland had opened in 1836), and by the end of the century the annual trade was worth £25,000. Miss Lambert gives a rather pretty lacy pattern for a Shetland shawl, which is very simple and quick to knit, no doubt reflecting the recent fashion for Shetland shawls in London.

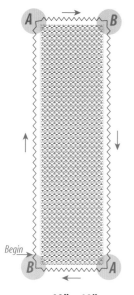

19" x 60"

10cm/4"

30

22

• over stockinette stitch
(knit on RS, purl on WS)

1 2 3 4 5 6

• **Super Fine weight**
700 yds

3.5mm/US 4, or size to obtain
gauge, 60cm (24") or longer

Two 3.5mm/US 4

&

• stitch markers
• blunt needle

Shown in handspun gray merino
Alternate yarns: LORNA'S LACES
Helen's Lace
JADE SAPPHIRE Cashmere 2-Ply or
KARABELLA Light-weight Cashmere

Miss Lambert's
Shetland pattern for a shawl

Corner A
Work 2 Single Joins (SJ), 2 Double Joins (DJ)—1 repeat of Chart B.
Work 2 DJ on long side, 1 DJ on short side—1 repeat of Chart B.
Work 2 DJ, 2 SJ—1 repeat of Chart B.

Corner B
Work 2 SJ, 2 DJ—1 repeat of Chart B.
Work 1 DJ on short side, 2 DJ on long side—1 repeat of Chart B.
Work 2 DJ, 2 SJ—1 repeat of Chart B.

Note
See *Techniques*, page 166, for lace cast-ons, S2KP2, knitted-on border
(including Single Join and Double Join), grafting, and blocking.

CENTER PANEL
Using a lace cast-on, cast on 71 stitches (multiple of 6 + 5) onto circular
needle. **Next row** Slip 1 purlwise with yarn at wrong side (sl 1), knit 2
together, knit to end—70 stitches.

Work 8-row repeat of Chart A marking last stitch of Row 3 of second
repeat and working chart a total of 48 times. Leave stitches on circular
needle. Cut yarn.

BORDER
Work knitted-on border Using a lace cast-on, cast on 7 stitches onto
double-pointed needle (dpn).
Beginning at marked slip stitch at left edge of center panel, * work 12-
row repeat of Chart B 30 times, working 6 Single Joins for each repeat.
Continue working Chart B, joining border to center panel as follows: Work
Corner A. [Work 6 Single Joins—1 repeat of Chart B] 10 times. Work
Corner B. Repeat from *, placing 70 loops from cast-on edge onto circular
needle before starting Corner A.
Place loops from border cast-on edge onto free dpn. Cut yarn and graft
ends together.

Block piece to measurements.

Chart A, Shetland pattern

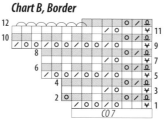

— 6-st repeat —
11 times

Chart B, Border

	K on RS, p on WS
	K on WS
O	Yo
/	K2tog
△	S2KP2
V	Slip st purlwise with yarn at WS
↓	Slip st purlwise with yarn at RS
Ω	K border st tbl tog with 1 center panel st
⌒	Bind off 1 st

Historic note
This Shetland pattern would probably have been
used for the center of a square shawl with a wavy
border in garter stitch stripes, as used on the
'cottage shawls' worn by the Shetlanders. Pattern
names varied according to locality: Miss Lambert's
Shell Pattern (Shetland) was later corrupted to Old
Shale (intended as pattern in sand left by waves)
and also called Feather Pattern by Jane Gaugain.

I have made a large rectangular shawl and added
Miss Lambert's only border, almost identical to
Mrs. Gaugain's (see Historic note, page 21). *My
Knitting Book* contains the two extra rows, added
by an unknown knitter to my copy of *The Lady's
Assistant*. Could it be that Miss Lambert had added
these two rows to Mrs. Gaugain's Knit Edging, and
renamed it Vandyke Border Pattern to avoid

accusations of plagiarism? Miss Lambert does
seem to have been very sensitive about this issue,
since she complains of piracy with regard to her
own patterns. Here, the term Vandyke describes
lace edging with deep triangular points, similar to
the lace collars in sixteenth-century portraits by Sir
Anthony Vandyke.

While perusing *Weldon's Practical Knitter, Vol. 1*, 1886, I discovered a leaf and trellis pattern described thus: "This is a very favourite old pattern for window curtains, cotton antimacassars, bread tray cloths and other articles. It is here rearranged and improved, and the veining of the leaves is carried symmetrically upwards." Intrigued, I tried it out, and found it to be Miss Lambert's leaf and trellis extended from a 20 to a 43-stitch repeat with added decreases and yarn-overs to give definition. How exciting to see the evolution of such a lovely pattern!

Large rectangle
in leaf and trellis pattern with trellis border

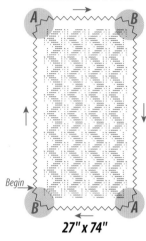

27" x 74"

10cm/4"

26

18

• over stockinette stitch
(knit on RS, purl on WS)

1 **2** 3 4 5 6

• *Fine weight*
1200 yds

4.5mm/US 7, or size to obtain
gauge, 60cm (24") or longer

Two 4mm/US 6

&
• stitch markers
• blunt needle
• small amount of smooth yarn for
cast-on

Shown in Handspun merino/
cashmere
Alternate yarns: NEEDFUL/LANA
GATTO Mohair Royal or JADE
SAPPHIRE Cahsmere 2-Ply

Corner A

Work 5 Single Joins (SJ), 2 Double Joins (DJ)—1 repeat of Chart B.
Work 3 DJ, 1 Triple Join (TJ)—1 repeat of Chart B.
Work 2 TJ on long side, 1 TJ on short side—1 repeat of Chart B.
Work 4 DJ, 1 SJ—1 repeat of Chart B.

Corner B

Work 1 SJ, 4 DJ—1 repeat of Chart B.
Work 1 TJ on short side, 2 TJ on long side—1 repeat of Chart B.
Work 1 TJ, 3 DJ—1 repeat of Chart B.
Work 2 DJ, 5 SJ—1 repeat of Chart B.

Note

See *Techniques*, page 166, for lace cast-ons, SSK, SK2P, knitted-on border
(including Single Join, Double Join, and Triple Join), grafting, and blocking.

CENTER PANEL

Using a lace cast-on, cast on 94 stitches (multiple of 43 + 8) onto
circular needle.

Next row Slip 1 purlwise with yarn at WS (sl 1), knit to end of row.
Work Chart A, Rows 1–18. Repeat Rows 3–18, marking last stitch in row
9 of second repeat and working chart A a total of 30 times.
Next row Sl 1, k2tog, knit to end—93 stitches.
Cut yarn.

BORDER

Work knitted-on border Using a lace cast-on, cast on 20 stitches onto
double-pointed needle (dpn).
Beginning at marked slip stitch at left edge of center panel, * work 18-row
repeat of Chart B 24 times, working 9 Single Joins for each repeat.
Continue working Chart B, joining border to center panel as follows:
Work Corner A. [Work 9 Single Joins—1 repeat of Chart B] 9 times.
Work Corner B. Repeat from *, placing 93 loops from cast-on edge onto
circular needle before starting Corner A.
Pick up loops from border cast-on edge onto free dpn. Cut yarn and graft
ends together.

Block piece to measurements.

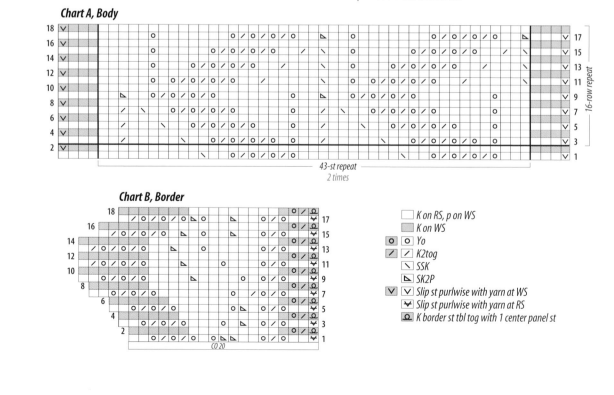

Chart A, Body

Chart B, Border

K on RS, p on WS
K on WS
○ Yo
∕ K2tog
∖ SSK
◣ SK2P
∨ Slip st purlwise with yarn at WS
⌄ Slip st purlwise with yarn at RS
⚺ K border st tbl tog with 1 center panel st

Very large shawls were popular by the 1840's, partly because they needed to be worn over increasingly wide skirts. The thick knitted shawl of the working class woman provided warmth and protection against the elements; the upper-class woman's Kashmiri shawl was a chic accessory and welcome protection against the draughty rooms of her house. Some knitted shawls were lined for extra warmth. At the Great Exhibition of 1851, over two dozen countries exhibited shawls, showing the level of demand for, and production of, these items.

In the course of a rummage in an antique shop, I came upon a truly magnificent handspun shawl constructed in the Shetland manner and measuring about six feet by four feet. At first glance it looked incredibly complicated, but on closer examination it was shown to consist of different patterns in horizontal strips, with an all-round border added on afterwards. I decided to design a sampler shawl in order to display some of the work of Jane Gaugain and Frances Lambert, using their methods of construction. Its many patterns produce a record of their time and give those new to lace knitting a learning experience.

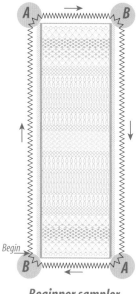

Begin

Beginner sampler
25" x 75"
Framed sampler
36" x 90"

10cm/4"
32
24

**• over stockinette stitch
(knit on RS, purl on WS)**

1 2 3 4 5 6

• Super Fine weight
Beginner Sampler 1650 yds
Framed Sampler 2850 yds

3.25mm/US 3, or size to obtain
gauge, 60cm (24") or longer

Two 3.25mm/US 2

&

• stitch markers
• blunt needle

JADE SAPPHIRE Lacey Lamb
2 balls in 20 soft pink
Framed sampler shown in 20/2 silk
Alternate yarn: LORNA'S LACES
Helen's Lace

Two sampler shawls
An 1840 heirloom

Corner A
Work 4 Single Joins (SJ), 1 Double Join (DJ)—1 repeat of Chart J.
Work 2 DJ on long side, 1 DJ on short side—1 repeat of Chart J.
Work 1 DJ, 4 SJ—1 repeat of Chart J.

Corner B
Work 4 SJ, 1 DJ—1 repeat of Chart J.
Work 1 DJ on short side, 2 DJ on long side—1 repeat of Chart J.
Work 1 DJ, 4 SJ—1 repeat of Chart J.

Note
1 See *Techniques*, page 166, for lace cast-ons, k3tog, SK2P, SSK, SSP, knitted-on border (including Single Join, Double Join, and Triple Join), and blocking.

PINK SAMPLER, CENTER PANEL
Using a lace cast-on, cast on 145 stitches onto circular needle.
Next row Slip 1 purlwise with yarn at WS (sl 1), k2tog, knit to end—144 stitches.
Next 7 rows Sl 1, knit to end.
Work Chart A, Rows 1–8—145 stitches.
Place markers (pm) between bracketed sections of chart: 6 garter stitches, pm, 4 faggoting stitches, pm, 125 center stitches, pm, 4 faggoting stitches, pm, 6 garter stitches.
Maintain established garter/faggoting patterns on first and last 10 stitches while working Center Pattern Sequence (see page 60) over center 125 stitches, marking last stitch of Row 1 of Chart B.
End by working Chart A, Rows 5–8, then Rows 1–4.
Next 7 rows Sl 1, knit to end.
Next row Sl 1, k2tog, knit to end—144 stitches.
Leave stitches on circular needle. Cut yarn.

BORDER
Work knitted-on border Using a lace cast-on, cast on 7 stitches onto double-pointed needle (dpn). Beginning at marked slip stitch at left edge of center panel, * work 12-row repeat of Chart J 50 times, working 6 Single Joins for each repeat.
Continue working Chart J, joining border to center panel as follows: Work Corner A. [Work 6 Single Joins—1 repeat of Chart B] 22 times.

Work Corner B. Repeat from *, placing 144 loops from cast-on edge onto circular needle before starting Corner A.
Place loops from border cast-on edge onto free dpn. Cut yarn and graft ends together.

Block piece to measurements.

CREAM SAMPLER, CENTER PANEL
Using a lace cast-on, cast on 211 stitches onto circular needle.
Next 8 rows Slip1 purlwise with yarn at WS (sl 1), knit to end.
Work 16-row repeat of Chart K, Diamond border, 2 times, marking last stitch of Row 9 of first repeat.
Work Chart L, Rows 1–6.
Place markers (pm) between bracketed sections of chart: 6 garter stitches, pm, 37 diamond border stitches, pm, 125 center stitches, pm, 37 diamond border stitches, pm, 6 garter stitches.
Maintain established garter/diamond patterns on first and last 43 stitches by completing Rows 7–16 of Chart L, then repeating Row 1–16, while working Center Pattern Sequence (see page 60).
Notes Center pattern rows and side border rows do not share row numbers. Remember to keep a note of the row numbers of both patterns, or use a separate magnet board for each lace. (I find it useful to pencil a line under the last row knitted when I take a break.) End by working 16-row repeat of Chart K 2 times.
Next 7 rows Sl 1, knit to end.
Next row Sl 1, k2tog, knit to end—210 stitches.
Leave stitches on circular needle. Cut yarn.

Cream Sampler Border
Work as pink sampler EXCEPT long sides have 60 border repeats between corners, and top and bottom have 33 border repeats between corners (placing 210 loops from cast-on edge onto circular needle before starting second Corner A).

Block piece to measurements.

Legend:
- ☐ K on RS, p on WS
- ▨ K on WS
- ⦿ Yo
- ╱ K2tog
- ◣ SK2P
- ☑ ∨ Slip st purlwise with yarn at WS
- ↘ Slip st purlwise with yarn at RS
- ⛬ K border st tbl tog with 1 center panel st
- ⌒ Bind off 1 st

Chart A, Frame

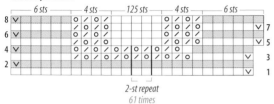

2-st repeat
61 times

Chart J, Vandyke border

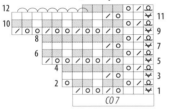

CO 7

Chart K, Diamond border, Gaugain

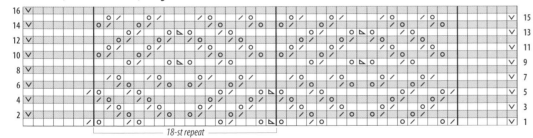

18-st repeat
10 times

As in the original, this wonderful 'real lace' pattern (every row patterned), has no directional decreases. When worked with directional decreases, it no longer looks 'old'.

Chart L, Side borders

Begin Center Pattern Sequence

2-st repeat
58 times

59

Center Pattern Sequence

LINKS All center patterns are separated by LINKS A or B.

LINK A 4 rows of stockinette stitch.

LINK B 6 rows of LINK B chart (used on cream sampler only).

10-row repeat of Chart B 1 time, LINK A (for pink sampler) or B (for cream sampler),
20-row repeat of Chart C 1 time, LINK A or B,
12-row repeat of Chart D 1 time, LINK A or B,
8-row repeat of Chart E 3 times, LINK A or B,
12-row repeat of Chart D 1 time, LINK A or B,
20-row repeat of Chart C 1 time, LINK A or B,
8-row repeat of Chart F 2 times, LINK A (for both samplers),
14-row repeat of Charts G 2 times, LINK A,
8-row repeat of Chart F 1 time, LINK A,
24-row repeat of Chart H 2 times, LINK A,
8-row repeat of Chart F 1 time, LINK A,
14-row repeat of Chart G 2 times, LINK A,
8-row repeat of Chart F 2 times, LINK A,
12-row repeat of Chart I four times—center pattern of shawl; mark and work preceding charts in reverse order for second half of shawl.

LINK B Chart

2-st repeat
58 times

Chart D, Medium leaf, Gaugain

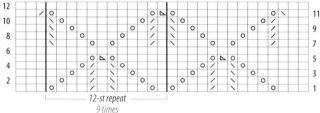

12-st repeat
9 times

All rows of Charts D and E are patterned; this type of pattern is known as 'knitted lace'.

Chart C, Large leaf, Gaugain

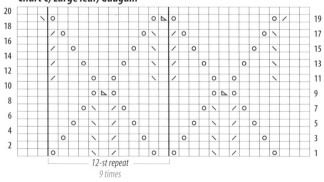

12-st repeat
9 times

The Victorians were obsessed with nature, especially plants. Each of the three leaf patterns (Charts C, D, and E) is pretty on its own, but together they complete the picture.

Chart B, Small diamond, Gaugain

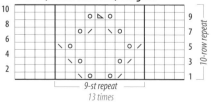

9-st repeat
13 times

10-row repeat

Wrong-side rows of Charts B, C, F, G, H, and I are purled; this type of pattern is known as 'lace knitting'.

60

Chart I, Open pattern, Gaugain

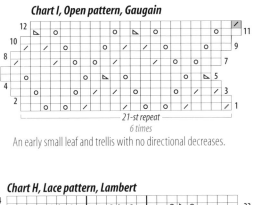

- ☐ K on RS, p on WS
- ▨ P on RS, k on WS
- ⊙ Yo
- ▨ On fourth repeat of chart, p2tog; on other repeats, purl
- ╱ K2tog on RS, p2tog on WS
- ╱ On first repeat of chart, knit; on other repeats, k2tog
- ╲ SSK on RS, SSP on WS
- ◿ P3tog
- ◺ SK2P

21-st repeat
6 times

An early small leaf and trellis with no directional decreases.

Chart H, Lace pattern, Lambert

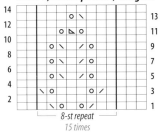

6-st repeat
18 times

This is point pattern stretched to its limits —and fun to knit!

Chart G, Scotch pattern, Gaugain

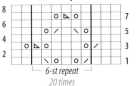

8-st repeat
15 times

This perfect illustration of how lace patterns grew and developed is simply point pattern in elongated form, but it looks quite different when knitted.

Chart F, Point pattern, Lambert

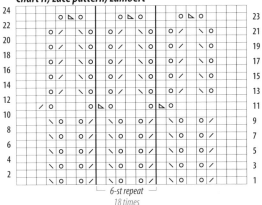

6-st repeat
20 times

Point pattern forms the building blocks of many later patterns. This is probably an old stocking pattern, also named 'spider pattern' by Mrs. Gaugain: simple, quick, and easy to follow.

Chart E, Small leaf, Lambert

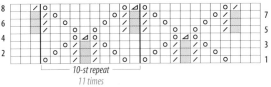

10-st repeat
11 times

This delightfully delicate pattern is a pattern in transition. Reverse stockinette stitches now appear between two sets of decreases for added definition, as in much later patterns, but without directional decreases.

Cornelia Mee was born in Bath, the daughter of a haberdasher, bookseller, and undertaker who had moved from London. In Victorian terms, the family were 'in trade' and probably very comfortably off, though Cornelia's mother died when she was 13, and her father a year later, leaving seven children. In 1837 Cornelia married Charles Mee and together (like Mrs. Gaugain and her husband) they ran a Berlin warehouse/ needlework shop at 41 Milsom Street in Bath. The Mees had now become importers of yarns, materials, and patterns from abroad. This must have been a good location for The Bath Emporium, the "Parisian Depot for the importation of Cashmeres" (very large Indian shawls), was nearby. Also, Jane Austen's General Tilney lodged on Milsom Street.

In 1842 and 1843 Cornelia published the *Manual of Knitting Netting and Crochet Work*. Only 28 of the 137 receipts are for knitting (her main interest lay in crochet). A second volume of 1842 indicates a considerable export trade in patterns and materials. "The Authoress presents this volume to the Ladies of the Empire who patronise the worktable as an humble attempt to simplify their labours, and with assurance that much that is novel and interesting will be found in its pages."

On the whole Cornelia Mee's patterns are practical designs for busy women, rather than purely decorative fashion items, and though, just like her contemporaries, she recommended size 20 needles (0.914mm) for fine edgings, she tended to favor larger needles and thicker wool for quicker production. She was very much a woman of today, entrepreneurial and aware of the difficulties of fitting a busy lifestyle around a large family.

The patterns in her early manuals were not reliable, and in my copy there are several handwritten corrections for German Lace, by a knitter. This appeared twice under different names and written in different styles, which probably indicates that the author had collected and printed these without trying them first.

On the whole, plain stitches were used. An interesting insight into stitch development was her description of SK2P–"slip1, k1, psso, put stitch back onto LH needle, slip next stitch over it, and replace on RH needle."

Her edging was the same as that of Miss Lambert and Mrs. Gaugain; her shawl designs favor stripes, checkerboard patterns, (intarsia) and plenty of color (one was knitted in a Fair Isle pattern with the yarn carried at the back), mainly using plain stitches. Others used faggoting, a slip stitch pattern given by all the early writers, and a simple diamond pattern. The most interesting for me was a shawl in "Chené of a most elegant appearance, almost like shaded velvet" in "scarlet, brown, pink, orange, blue, gray, green, white and yellow." This yarn was described as shaded, and appears to have consisted of different colored plies. In any event, it only required plain knitting (garter stitch) and a riot of color to gain the desired effect. As an example of pretty typical early pattern instructions see the following from the 8–page instructions for "Open Vandyke pattern for a scarf"

–row 8. "seam 6, make seam 2tog, make 1 seam 2 tog, make 1 seam 2tog, seam 1 seam 2tog, seam 2 tog, seam 2 tog, make 1 seam 7, make 1 seam 2tog, make 1 seam 2tog, make 1 seam 2tog, seam 1 seam 2tog, make 1 seam 2tog, seam 2 tog, make 1 seam 7, make 1, seam 2tog, make 1 seam 2tog, make 1 seam 2tog, seam 1 seam 2tog, seam 2tog, seam 2tog, make 1 seam 7, make 1 seam 2tog, make 1 seam 2tog, make 1 seam 2tog, seam 1 seam 2tog, seam 2tog, seam 2tog, make 1 seam 7, make 1
seam 2tog, make 1 seam 2tog, make 1 seam 2 tog, seam 1 seam 2tog, seam 2tog, seam 2tog, make 1 seam 7, make 1 seam 2tog, make 1 seam 2tog, seam 2tog, seam 2tog, seam 1 seam 2tog, seam 2tog, seam 2tog make 1 seam 6…..

And it gets worse! Most early writers did not abbreviate anything–not even *together*. Cornelia published a number of knitting Manuals, and her sister Mary worked with her from 1848.

A *Manual of Needlework* was published in 1854 and it was here that I found a beautiful veil which appears to be in French or Spanish style, and although it is described as a Shetland Veil (page 68) the title may refer to the fineness of yarn and current fashion for Shetland shawls, rather than the actual origin of the pattern. (R.Rutt–'History of Knitting'–states that Shetland shawls were superseded by veils around 1850).

The *Alliance Book of Knitting Netting and Crochet* appeared in 1856 as a very thin volume (economy edition) in response to the Crimean war in which England and France helped Turkey to resist Russian occupation. "The increasing demand for Novelties in Work, especially Knitting, has induced me to bring out this Publication, to make it useful to all classes of workers, . . ." and, possibly in response to earlier complaints of inaccuracy, "No pattern is published that has not been tested by experienced workers . . .". Cornelia regarded herself as a teacher of some repute, and operated her own customer service policy as well as publishing her work abroad "any difficulty [could be] explained to the Ladies or Workers at a distance, by sending a stamped and directed envelope." Also, since cotton yarn by Walter Evans & Co was recommended in the book, it is probable that they paid her for the advertisement, or sponsored the publication of the book, and supplied her with yarn samples.

Mee

Receipts included a Crimea Cap "a great number of these were sent out to the Crimea last year and afforded great comfort to the brave soldiers there." There was also a nine-page-long lace pattern for a knitted curtain, and another for window blinds, based on faggoting.

In 1858 the Mees moved to Regent Street, London, while at the same time keeping in touch with clients in Bath. They later progressed to an even better address in Brook Street. *The Queen's Winter Knitting Book* was published in 1862, as a third series of *The Knitters Companion*, and yet another encouragement to ladies' charity work.

The Preface states that "So many applications having been made for rules for making warm things for the poor in Lancashire; this little book has been hastily arranged in an inexpensive form to meet the wishes of many benevolent ladies who are occupying their time in working for the distressed operatives; hoping that it may assist them in their labour of love."

At this time there was considerable unemployment and poverty in Lancashire, England, because the American Civil War had halted the cotton trade. No raw cotton was being imported, and the mills were out of action. It is interesting to see how much the fortunes of English factory workers depended on America. At the same time, American women were knitting for their soldiers in the Civil War.

I loved the descriptions of "children's Bootakins", Siberian cuffs, "porcupine knitting for a bag," and "gentlemen's braces.' When Cornelia Mee died in 1875, her daughter Agnes kept the business going until about 1890, by which time about 300,000 copies of her books had been sold (R.Rutt).

Branchardière

Despite her title, Mlle. Riego de la Branchardière was actually English, with an Irish mother and a French father (an aristocrat exiled from France by the Revolution).

Although she won a medal for crochet at the Great Exhibition in 1851 and another in 1852, her first publication was a knitting book in 1847. It explained how to knit and was apparently aimed at novice knitters. Previous authors had assumed that their readers were at least familiar with circular stocking knitting; Miss Lambert had even told knitters how to hold their needles elegantly.

In 1860, *The Andalusian Knitting and Netting Book* was published. The book has no index or contents, and consists mainly of crochet patterns, many with French names (which coincidentally was the height of fashion), together with a few practical knitting patterns, such as one for a baby's shoe and sock, a gentleman's cravat, and cuffs. For the first time in my research, there are color illustrations.

In 1861, a *Book of Siberian Wool* (with illustrations in red) gave, for the first time that I am aware, detailed requirements for yarn and needles; for example, calling for 2 ounces of wool for every square foot! From the title, it would appear that sponsorship from wool manufacturers (rather than from the aristocracy as in earlier times) was shaping the knitting publications.

In the same year, there was another book, *Melange de Laine for Siberian and Leviathon Wools*. New yarns were available, some thicker and more fluffy in texture and with a greater variety of colors to choose from. One pattern was for an antimacassar in blue, gray, and gold; another for a couvre pieds [lap robe], and two designs for quilts which were based on six and eight-pointed stars—echoes of Jane Gaugain's Cap Shawl (see page 26).

Also in 1861, three small books on *Waved Crochet Braid* and yet another on *Waved Trimmings* in 1862, which Mlle. declared was "the last I will write until the Spring"! She was by then busy preparing new designs for the International Exhibition, at which she won a Gold Medal. One of the designs, for some Greek lace trimming, was exquisite, and appeared later that year in Mlle. Riego's *Crochet Book* together with a Vine Pattern and Medieval Rose Antimacassar "in imitation of old Spanish and other costly laces."

In 1867, *The Abergeldie Winter Book*, measuring 5¾ by 4¾ inches, was published. The title may refer to Abergeldie Castle in Scotland, leased by The Prince Consort for Albert, Prince of Wales (later Edward VII), or it could just be a reference to Royal connections and patronage, as Mlle. was "by special appointment Artiste in Needlework" to HRH The Princess of Wales.

This book appears in part to be a re-print of some of the material from *The Andalusian Knitting Book* of 1860. The beautiful illustrations appear again in red, green, and white, of an opera hood, petticoat, vest, cape, muff, and 'crossover' (see illustration). It is a truly delightful little book, and also contains the pattern for A Round Shetland Veil. This is actually a half-circle with diamond edging and a remarkably modern appearance (see page 70).

I was unable to discover whether Mlle. was married, but in the knowledge that Miss Lambert was married, prefer to keep an open mind on the subject. It is likely that she was a lady of ample means, who may have been able to support herself. Certainly her prolific writing and Exhibition entries would indicate that she was a dedicated career-woman.

Lace was ubiquitous throughout the 19th century, appearing everywhere about the lady's person. Trims were common on collars and cuffs—either handmade or (by mid-century) the widely available machine-made lace. Entire dresses were made out of this intensely feminine cloth, and the popularity of such styles continued unabated through the century. Lace shawls were in keeping with these fashions, and the expanse of the shawl allowed the beauty of the lace design to shine through to its best effect. This veil pattern is an excellent example of delicate knitted lace.

Cornelia Mee's Knitted veil is layered under the Myrtle leaf shawl from page 140—sometimes one shawl just isn't enough.

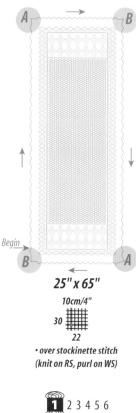

25" x 65"

10cm/4"

30 [grid] **22**
• *over stockinette stitch (knit on RS, purl on WS)*

1 2 3 4 5 6
• *Super Fine weight*
1300 yds

3.5mm/US 4, or size to obtain gauge, 60cm (24") or longer

[needles]

Two 3.5mm/US 4, or size to obtain gauge

&
• stitch markers
• blunt needle

Shown in 2-ply merino handspun
Alternate yarns: ALPACA WITH A TWIST Fino or MISTI ALPACA Lace

A knitted veil
in Pyrenees wool

From *The Manual of Needlework*, Cornelia Mee, London, 1854. Since this pattern was for a veil the diamonds appeared at one end only. In order to update it as a scarf I added a balancing set of diamonds at the opposite end.

Corner A

Work 3 Single Joins, (SJ), 2 Double Joins (DJ)—1 repeat of Chart B.
Work 1 DJ, 1 Triple Join (TJ) on long side, 1 DJ on short side—1 repeat of Chart B.
Work 1 DJ, 5 SJ—1 repeat of Chart B.

Corner B

Work 5 SJ, 1 DJ—1 repeat of Chart B.
Work 1 DJ on short side, 1 TJ, 1 DJ on long side—1 repeat of Chart B.
Work 2 DJ, 3 SJ—1 repeat of Chart B.

Note

See *Techniques*, page 166, for lace cast-ons, knitted-on border (including Single Join, Double Join, and Triple Join), grafting, and blocking.

CENTER PANEL

Using a lace cast-on, cast on 113 stitches onto circular needle.
Diamond border Work Chart A, Rows 1–12.
Double-diamond center with faggotting frame and right and left diamond borders Work Chart A, Rows 13–66, marking last stitch of Row 15.
*Chart A, rows 67–70 Work 12 stitches of diamond border and 3 stitches of faggoting; work next 83 stitches (6-stitch repeat + 5 stitches of small center pattern); work 3 stitches of faggoting and 12 stitches of diamond border.
Rows 71–102 Continue as established; the last 36 rows produce two 18-row repeats of diamond border and nine 4-row repeats of small center pattern. Repeat from * for a total of 8 repeats, ending with completion of both center and border patterns. If more length is desired, work two more 18 row repeats of border with nine more 4 row repeats of small center pattern.

Work Chart A, Rows 13–66.
Work Chart A, Rows 3–12.
Work Chart A, Rows 1–2, working knit 2 together after the slip stitch in Row 2—112 stitches.
Leave stitches on circular needle. Cut yarn.

BORDER

Work knitted-on border Using a lace cast-on, cast on 10 stitches onto double-pointed needle (dpn).
Beginning at marked slip stitch at left edge of center panel, * work 14-row repeat of Chart B 28 times, working 7 Single Joins for each repeat. Continue working Chart B, joining border to center panel as follows:
Work Corner A. [Work 7 Single Joins—1 repeat of Chart B] 14 times. Work Corner B. Repeat from *, placing 112 loops from cast-on edge onto circular needle before starting Corner A.
Place loops from border cast-on edge onto free dpn. Cut yarn and graft ends together.

Block piece to measurements.

Chart A, Shawl

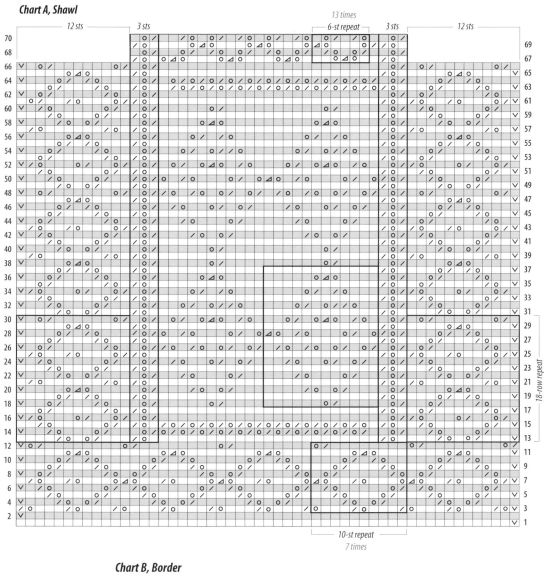

Chart B, Border

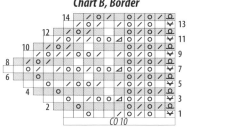

Legend:

- ☐ K on RS, p on WS
- ☐ K on WS
- ○ Yo
- ╱ K2tog
- ◿ K3tog
- ∨ Slip st purlwise with yarn at WS
- ⊻ Slip st purlwise with yarn at RS
- ⚷ K border st tbl tog with 1 center panel st

Understanding lace

If, like me, you wonder how much center pattern to knit before beginning the second diamond panel, do a preliminary blocking. Put all stitches onto a long circular needle, wet the fabric within a couple of inches of the needle; gently squeeze out excess water and roll in a towel. Block out the damp knitting and measure it. If lower border including diamonds = 12", and one center block = 7", by adding 12" for a second border, it is possible to work out how many repeats of the center pattern are desired. Remember that additional width and length is added all around when the border is knitted on.

Scarf option

For a scarf, cast on 53 stitches. On Rows 67–70, center 3 repeats of small pattern over 25 stitches.

This shawl has a surprisingly contemporary appearance, you could even try it with bigger needles to exaggerate its open pattern.

When I saw the illustration of this shawl in Mlle. de la B's *The Abergeldie Winter Book*, I knew I had seen it somewhere before, and eventually tracked it down: A Semicircular Scarf in Spider Pattern in Sarah Don's book, *The Art of Shetland Lace* is "a copy of a scarf found in an old box of knitting discovered recently at Unst" [Shetland, pre-1980]. Its center pattern and that of 1860 are identical, but the borders are totally different. The 1860 border has 16 rows, and Don's version has 12 rows. The other difference is in construction. Don's shawl begins with the border which is later grafted onto the center. This Spider pattern bears no resemblance to that of Jane Gaugain.

A curved shawl
with diamond edging

21" x 62"

10cm/4"
40 | 24
• over garter stitch
(knit all rows)

1 2 3 4 5 6
• Super fine weight
750 yds

3.25mm/US 3, or size to obtain
gauge, 60cm (24") or longer

Two 3.25mm/US 3

&
• stitch markers
• blunt needle

JADE SAPPHIRE Lacey Lamb 1 ball
in 225 Blueblood Red

Notes
1 See *Techniques*, page 166, for loop cast-on, S2KP2, knitted-on border (including Single Join and Double Join), and blocking. *2* For a longer and wider shawl, each additional 4-row/6-stitch repeat of Chart A adds approximately ¾" to length and 1¼" to width. This stitch grows wide very quickly; reduce the number of stitches cast on if you wish a deep shawl. *3* If preferred, border can be sewn on, attaching 4 border rows to each loop along curved edge.

CENTER
Using loop cast-on, cast on 49 stitches .
Work Chart A, Rows 1–12—67 stitches.
Note Three 4-row repeats of pattern have been worked. Every 4-row repeat begins and ends the same; the only difference is the number of 6-stitch repeats. Every 4 rows, 6 stitches are increased, adding one additional repeat.
Continue working thus for a total of 168 rows (forty-two 4-row repeats)—301 stitches.
Next 8 rows Slip 1 purlwise with yarn at wrong side (sl 1), knit to end.
Picot bind-off * Cast on 2 stitches, bind off 5 stitches; repeat from *, ending bind off 2 stitches.

BORDER
Work knitted-on border Cast on 13 stitches onto double-pointed needle (dpn). Beginning at top right of center piece, work 16-row repeat of Chart B, working 4 Single Joins and 2 Double Joins.
Next 53 repeats Work Double Joins into each edge loop and cast-on loop—4 Double Joins for each repeat of Chart B.
Last repeat Work 2 Double Joins and 4 Single Joins. Bind off.

Block piece to measurements.

Chart A, Shawl

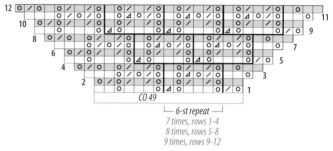

CO 49

└─ 6-st repeat ─┘
7 times, rows 1-4
8 times, rows 5-8
9 times, rows 9-12

Chart B, Border

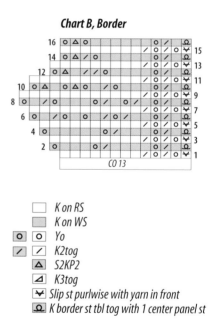

CO 13

	K on RS
	K on WS
o	Yo
/	K2tog
▲	S2KP2
◿	K3tog
⤵	Slip st purlwise with yarn in front
Ω	K border st tbl tog with 1 center panel st

Understanding lace
The original shawl pattern used a k3tog decrease instead of an S2KP2. Try both to see which you prefer. The Center patterns of Mee's Knitted Veil (page 69), and the Curved Shawl are nearly the same: the third row is different and the fourth row is shifted.

74

Wide-bordered scarves

The next, and very large, source of Victorian knitting patterns, the periodical *Weldon's Practical Needlework,* is the primary inspiration for the next two chapters. Weldon's 1890 knitting series was an explosion of lace—mainly borders. Some of these were very wide, really too wide for shawls unless the corners could be mitered. (Even knitted-on borders have their limitations.) So I had to be inventive, just as the Victorians had been.

Today, the best way to display very wide borders is to use them at the ends or at the sides of scarves. This not only displays the lace pattern full-on, it also eliminates the problem of corners. The repetitive part of the scarf—the long center pattern—can be as simple, or as complicated, as you wish. It is an excellent way for lace novices to sample and gain an understanding of different lace patterns. When exploring something new, variety is often a great stimulant to further adventures. Knitters can begin with the easiest scarf border (say the striped border on page 80) and progress gradually to some of the more complicated ones. If you take something in stages, it is usually do-able. Knitting a scarf is also a great way to try a yarn or fiber you haven't used before—silk, cashmere, bamboo—try them all. Often, it only takes a ball or two of something very luxurious for a scarf you will love knitting and wearing.

The sight of a newly blocked, wide silk border is truly amazing. If you can't wait to see the border before finishing the scarf, you can even block it while still on the needle—just to have a glimpse of what is to come. That will make you want to knit the middle section a great deal quicker.

The 1890 issue of Weldon's magazine contains several patterns for shawls, clouds, scarves, a fanchon and a fascinator—all using extremely simple stitches. One scarf or cloud was to be made on thick wooden pins in plain knitting (garter stitch), another was in twisted drop-stitch with three yarn-overs which was a bit too open, and others used very simple yarn-over patterns which produced a sort of netting fabric. None of these seemed quite suitable for today, but single drop-stitch combined with garter stitch works well, especially after blocking. The fabric has an almost woven appearance and creates the perfect center pattern for a modern scarf.

I developed the idea further using wide border patterns for the scarf ends. Many of the wider edgings are most attractive and can easily be adapted to suit changing taste, though some of the original names such as 'Wide and handsome border for a Mantel Drape' cannot! Some are perfect for knitting at both ends of a scarf only, without the extra work of an all-around border; others have been worked lengthwise with a central insertion.

As always with lace, blocking is essential. The scarf will look truly dreadful before blocking—but take heart, a transformation will take place. I never cease to be excited when blocking a piece; that is when the beauty of the lace pattern is revealed.

Eight of the eleven scarves that follow use this basic approach. In a another (page 84), the border pattern forms the sides of the scarf and the center pattern is only 15 rows. The last two scarves (pages 104 and 106) take a different approach; two borders and a central insertion are knitted in one operation. This method requires careful attention.

For even more choices, use this basic method to combine other lace patterns. Or, see 'How to make your own wide border' on pages 182 and 183.

Wide-bordered scarves
a basic approach

First border

1 Cast on stitches for the border. Since crochet cast-on resembles the bind-off, it is recommended (see page 167). * Knit (or purl) 1 row. Work the border pattern for the width of the scarf. Knit 1 row. **

2 Bind off at the same tension as you cast-on, placing the last stitch on a holder.

Cast on

Center of scarf

3 Turn work and pick up the slip stitches along the straight edge of the border, then return the stitch from the holder to the needle; the stitches for the center pattern are on the needle.

4 Work 1 wrong-side row, knitting (or purling) through the back loop of each stitch, and increasing or decreasing a few stitches if necessary for the center pattern repeat.

Work the center pattern to the desired length of the scarf less the second border, ending with a right-side row. (If it was necessary to increase or decrease for the center pattern, return to the original stitch number as you work this row.) Do not turn work.

Bind off

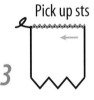

Pick up sts

Second border

5 Slip the first stitch from the needle onto a crochet hook. Crochet cast-on stitches for the border, and place the loop from the crochet hook onto the needle; the total stitches for scarf and border are on the needle.

Work as first border from * to **, EXCEPT work as knitted-on border, (on wrong-side rows, work last border stitch together with a shawl stitch, see page 174).

Bind off.

Block scarf.

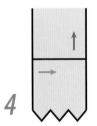

Bind off

Cast on

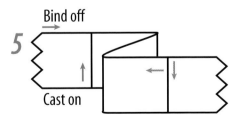

Scarf

with the striped border from *Weldon's, Volume 5*, 1890

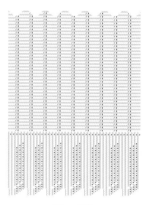

8" x 64"

10cm/4"

32

18

• **over garter stitch**
(knit all rows)

1 **2** 3 4 5 6

• **Fine weight**
400 yds

Straight or circular
4.5mm/US 7, or size to obtain gauge

&

• stitch markers
• blunt needle
• crochet hook for cast-on

Shown in hand-spun silk.
Almost any Fine weight or Light
weight yarn will work; remember,
a thicker yarn with bigger needles
will make a wider scarf.

Notes

1 See *Techniques*, page 166, for crochet cast-on, knitted-on border (including Single Join), and blocking.
2 Match the tension of the bind-off to the cast-on edge. *3* To make a narrower (or wider) scarf, work 2 fewer
(or more) 12-row repeats of Chart A for borders AND pick up 12 fewer (or more) stitches for center section.

First border

1 Crochet cast on 25 stitches. * Knit 1 row.
   Work 12-row repeat of Chart A seven times. Knit 1 row.**
2 Bind off, placing the last stitch on a holder.

Center of scarf

3 Turn work and pick up slip stitches along straight edge of border, then return stitch from holder to
   needle, for a total of 42 stitches.
4 **Next row** (WS) Knit through back loop of each stitch. Work 2-row repeat of Chart B to desired length
   less second border (scarf shown has 110 repeats). Knit 1 row. Do not turn work.

Second border

5 Slip first stitch from needle onto crochet hook and crochet cast on 25 stitches—67 stitches on needle
   (42 scarf stitches, 25 border stitches). Work as First border from * to **, working Chart A as knitted-
   on border. Bind off.

Block piece to measurements.

1 Cast on

Bind off
2

Pick up sts
3

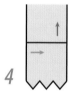
4

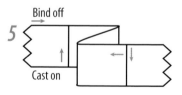
Bind off
5
Cast on

Chart A, Border

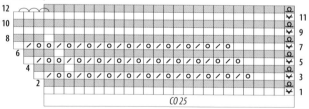

CO 25

Chart B, Scarf

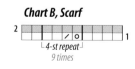

4-st repeat
9 times

☐ K on RS, p on WS
▨ K on WS
○ Yo
╱ K2tog
⊻ Slip st purlwise with yarn at RS
Ⓠ On first border, k tbl; on second border,
   k border st tbl tog with scarf st
⌢ Bind off 1 st

As the easiest of the wide borders, this is a good scarf to start with if you are new to lace knitting. This Striped Border is a simple version of the well-known Godmother's Edging, traditionally used to trim christening gowns, and is described as "of particularly pleasing appearance, being light and lacy, and yet not difficult of accomplishment."

Scarf

with the Clarence Border from *Weldon's*, 1886

10" x 64"

10cm/4"

32
18
• over garter stitch
(knit all rows)

1 **2** 3 4 5 6

• *Fine weight*
450 yds

Straight or circular
4.5mm/US 7, or size to obtain gauge

&
• stitch markers
• blunt needle
• crochet hook for cast-on

Shown in hand-spun silk
Almost any Fine or Light weight
yarn will work; remember, a
thicker yarn with bigger needles
will make a wider scarf.

Drop-stitch pattern

Knit 3 rows.

Row 1 Knit, wrapping yarn 2 times around needle.

Row 2 Knit, dropping extra wrap as stitch is pulled off left needle. (Rows 1 and 2 form elongated stitches.)

Rows 3–4 Knit.

Repeat Rows 1–4 for Drop-stitch pattern.

Notes

1 See *Techniques*, page 166, for crochet cast-on, knitted-on border (including Single Join), elongated stitch, and blocking. *2* Match the tension of the bind-off to the cast-on edge.

First border

1 Crochet cast on 34 stitches. * Knit 1 row. Work 40-row repeat of Chart A three times. Knit 1 row. **

2 Bind off, placing the last stitch on a holder.

Center of scarf

3 Turn work and pick up slip stitches along straight edge of border, then return stitch from holder to needle, for a total of 62 stitches.

4 *Next row* (WS) Knit through back loop of each stitch. Work 4-row repeat of Drop-stitch pattern to desired length less second border (scarf shown has 30 repeats). Knit 1 row. Do not turn work.

Second border

5 Slip first stitch from needle onto crochet hook and crochet cast on 34 stitches—96 stitches on needle (62 scarf stitches, 34 border stitches). Work as First border from * to **, working Chart A as knitted-on border. Bind off.

Block piece to measurements.

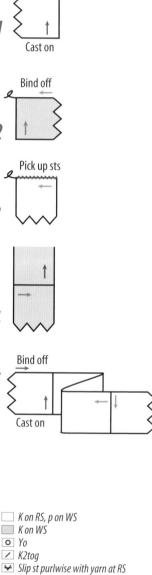

1 Cast on

2 Bind off

3 Pick up sts

4

5 Bind off / Cast on

Chart A, Clarence border

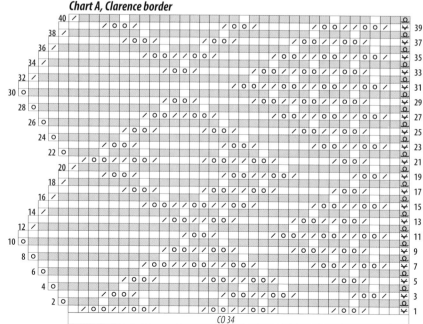

CO 34

☐ K on RS, p on WS
▨ K on WS
○ Yo
╱ K2tog
⋎ Slip st purlwise with yarn at RS
⚏ On first border, k tbl; on second border, k border st tbl tog with scarf st

"This is a wide handsome border for quilts, large shawls, or any large piece of work. The material and the knitting needles must be regulated to suit the article for which it is to be used."

— *Weldon's*

83

Scarf

with the No. 20 edging from The Knitted Lace Pattern Book, *Thompson Bros., Kilmarnock, Scotland, 1850*

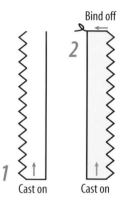

Bind off

Cast on   Cast on

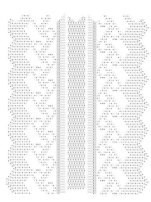

INTERMEDIATE LACE

20" x 72"

10cm/4"

26

18
• over stockinette stitch
(knit on RS, purl on WS)

1 **2** 3 4 5 6

• Fine weight
600 yds

4.5mm/US 7, or size to obtain
gauge, 60cm (24") or longer

4mm/G

&
• stitch markers
• blunt needle

NEEDFUL/LANA GATTO
Mohair Royal
3 balls in 2118

Notes

1 See *Techniques,* page 166, for crochet cast-on, knitted-on border (including Single Join), and blocking.
2 Match the tension of the bind-off to the cast-on edge. **3** The borders of this scarf run lengthwise with only a few rows of center pattern between the borders.

First border

1 Crochet cast on 30 stitches. * Purl 1 row.

Work 20-row repeat of Chart A twenty-two times. Knit 1 row. **

2 Bind off, placing the last stitch on a holder.

Center of scarf

3 Turn work and pick up slip stitches along straight edge of border, then return stitch from holder to needle, for a total of 222 stitches.

4 **Next row** (WS) Purl through back loop of each stitch.

Work 15 rows of Chart B. Do not turn work.

Second border

5 Slip first stitch from needle onto crochet hook and crochet cast on 30 stitches—252 stitches on needle (222 scarf stitches, 30 border stitches). Work as First border from * to **, working Chart A as knitted-on border. Bind off.

Work picot edging, Row 1 With crochet hook and right-side of scarf facing, single crochet (sc) into each stitch of borders and center pattern along one short end of scarf, ending with an even number of scs. **Row 2** * Chain 3, (sc into next sc) 2 times; repeat from *, end chain 3, sc into next sc. Repeat Rows 1 and 2 along other short end.

Block piece to measurements.

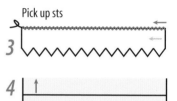
Pick up sts

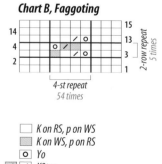
Cast on   Bind off

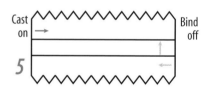

Chart B, Faggoting

14
4
2

15
13
3
1

2-row repeat
5 times

4-st repeat
54 times

☐ K on RS, p on WS
▨ K on WS, p on RS
○ Yo
⁄ K2tog
◣ SK2P
⟝ Slip st purlwise with yarn at RS
Ω On first border, k tbl; on second border, k border st tbl tog with scarf st

Chart A, Diamond border

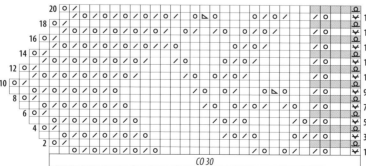

CO 30

84   VICTORIAN LACE TODAY

Scarf

with a wide and handsome border for a mantel
drape from *Weldon's, Series 6, Volume 2, 1887*

10" x 70"

10cm/4"

38
20

· over garter stitch
(knit all rows)

1 **2** 3 4 5 6

· **Fine weight**
480 yds

Straight or circular
3.75mm/US 5, or size to obtain
gauge

&

· stitch markers
· blunt needle
· crochet hook for cast-on

HABU 2/17 Tsumugi 1 cone
in 35 Whiskey

Drop-stitch pattern

Knit 3 rows.

Row 1 Knit, wrapping yarn 2 times around needle.

Row 2 Knit, dropping extra wrap as stitch
is pulled off left needle. (Rows 1 and 2 form
elongated stitches.)

Rows 3–4 Knit.

Repeat Rows 1–4 for Drop-stitch pattern.

Notes

1 See *Techniques*, page 166, for crochet cast-on,
knitted-on border (including Single Join),
elongated stitch, and blocking. *2* Match the
tension of the bind-off to the cast-on edge.

First border

1 Crochet cast on 36 stitches. * Knit 1 row.
Work 42-row repeat of Chart A three times. Knit
1 row. **

2 Bind off, placing the last stitch on a holder.

Center of scarf

3 Turn work and pick up slip stitches along straight
edge of border, then return stitch from holder to
needle, for a total of 65 stitches.

4 *Next row* (WS) Knit through back loop of each
stitch. Work 4-row repeat of Drop-stitch pattern
to desired length less second border (scarf shown
has 56 repeats). Knit 1 row. Do not turn work.

Second border

5 Slip first stitch from needle onto crochet hook
and crochet cast on 36 stitches—101 stitches
on needle (65 scarf stitches, 36 border stitches).
Work as First border from * to **, working Chart
A as knitted-on border. Bind off.

Block piece to measurements.

1
Cast on

Bind off

2

Pick up sts

3

4

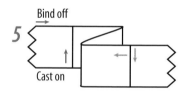
Bind off

5
Cast on

Chart A, Wide and handsome border

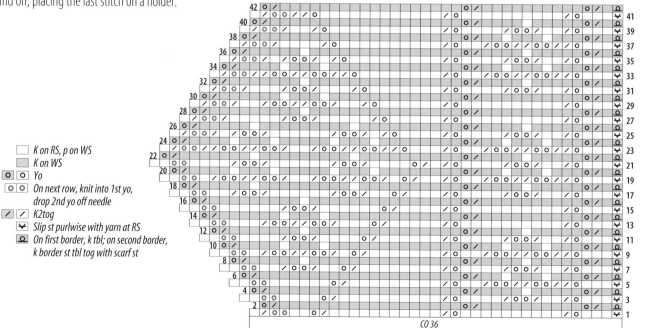

☐ K on RS, p on WS
▨ K on WS
⊙|⊙ Yo
⊙|⊙ On next row, knit into 1st yo,
drop 2nd yo off needle
╱|╱ K2tog
❤ Slip st purlwise with yarn at RS
Ω On first border, k tbl; on second border,
k border st tbl tog with scarf st

This splendid border is
stunning with either
the simple Drop-stitch
pattern shown here
or the Open diamond
insertion from page 91.

Scarf

with the open and solid diamond lace edging from *Weldon's, 1904*

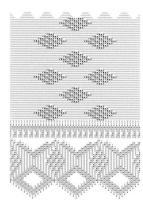

10" x 70"

10cm/4"

38

20

- **over garter stitch (knit all rows)**

1 **2** 3 4 5 6

- **Fine weight**
450 yds

Straight or circular
4.5mm/US 7, or size to obtain gauge

&

- stitch markers
- blunt needle
- crochet hook for cast-on

Shown in hand-dyed 2-ply silk
Alternate yarns: FIESTA La Luz or
HABU 2/10 Kusaki-Zome

Notes

1 See *Techniques*, page 166, for crochet cast-on, knitted-on border (including Single Join), and blocking. *2* Match the tension of the bind-off to the cast-on edge. *3* This insertion would also work with the Clarence border shown on page 82.

First border

1 Crochet cast on 32 stitches. * Knit 1 row. Work 32-row repeat of Chart A four times. Knit 1 row.**

2 Bind off, placing the last stitch on a holder.

Center of scarf

3 Turn work and pick up slip stitches along straight edge of border, then return stitch from holder to needle, for a total of 66 stitches.

4 ***Next row*** (WS) Knitting through back loop of each stitch, knit 13, place marker (pm), knit 40, pm, knit to end.
Establish garter-stitch borders and center insertion, next row Knit 13, work Chart B over 40 stitches, knit 13. Continue as established, working Chart B over center 40 stitches as follows: work Rows 1–32 six times, then Rows 1–16 once. Knit 1 row. Do not turn work.

Second border

5 Slip first stitch from needle onto crochet hook and crochet cast on 32 stitches—98 stitches on needle (66 scarf stitches, 32 border stitches). Work as First border from * to **, working Chart A as knitted-on border. Bind off.

Block piece to measurements.

Chart A, Diamond lace border

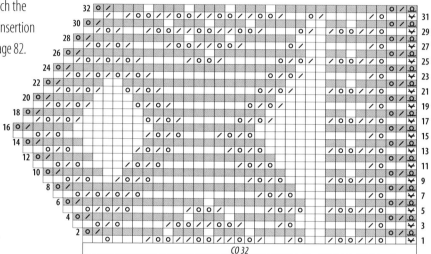

Chart B, Open diamond insertion

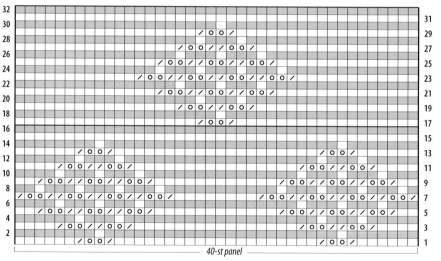

K on RS, p on WS
K on WS, p on RS
Yo
K2tog
Slip st purlwise with yarn at RS
On first border, k tbl; on second border, k border st tbl tog with scarf st

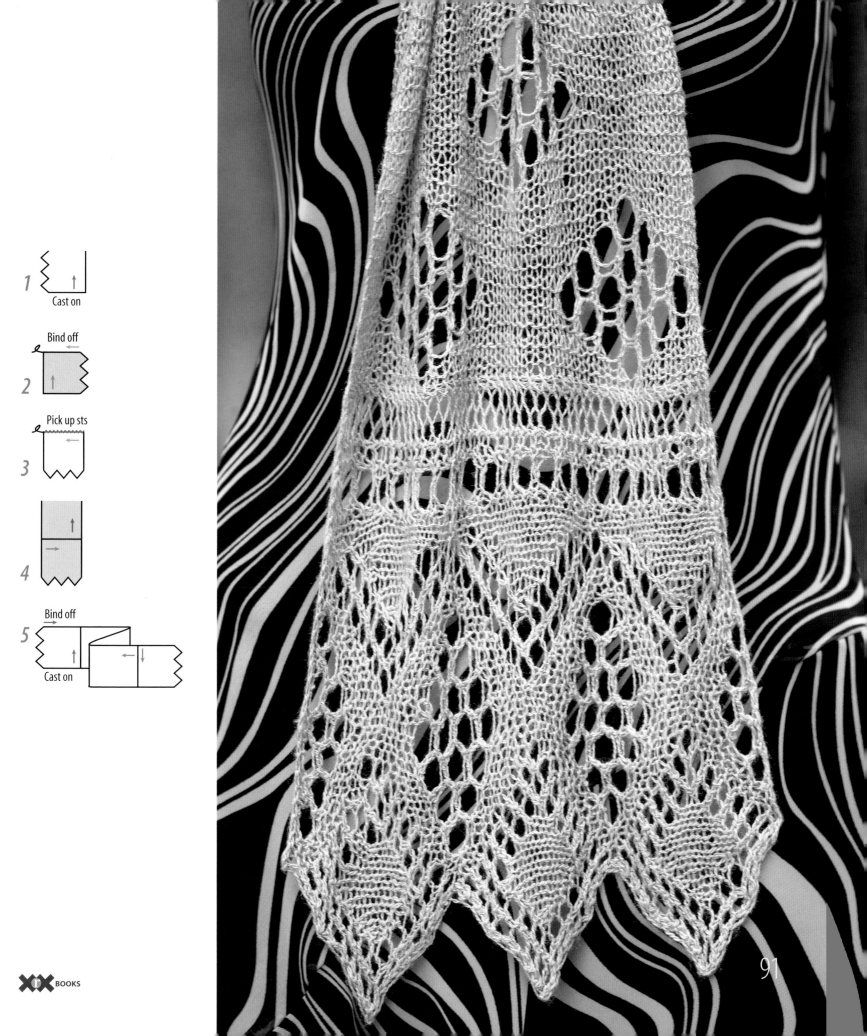

1 Cast on

2 Bind off

3 Pick up sts

4

5 Bind off
Cast on

91

Victorian ruby

derived from The Knitted Lace Pattern Book, Thompson Bros., Kilmarnack, Scotland, 1850

INTERMEDIATE LACE

13" x 78"

10cm/4"

32

18

• over garter stitch
(knit all rows)

1 **2** 3 4 5 6

• Fine weight
450 yds

Straight or circular
4.5mm/US 7, or
size to obtain gauge

• stitch markers
• blunt needle
• crochet hook for cast-on

ROWAN Kidsilk Haze
2 balls in 606 Candy Girl

Drop-stitch pattern

Knit 3 rows.

Row 1 Knit, wrapping yarn 2 times around needle.

Row 2 Knit, dropping extra wrap as stitch is pulled from left needle. (Rows 1 and 2 form elongated stitches.)

Rows 3–4 Knit.

Repeat Rows 1–4 for Drop-stitch pattern.

Notes

1 See *Techniques*, page 166, for crochet cast-on, S2KP2, knitted-on border (including Single Join), elongated stitch, and blocking.
2 Match the tension of the bind-off to the cast-on edge.

First border

1 Crochet cast on 45 stitches. * Knit 1 row.
Work Chart A, Rows 1–46, but do not knit the red symbols in the middle of Row 45. Repeat Chart A, Rows 15–58, but this time work the red symbols for lace in Row 45. Knit 1 row. **

2 Bind off, placing the last stitch on a holder.

Center of scarf

3 Turn work and pick up slip stitches along straight edge of border, then return stitch from holder to needle, for a total of 47 stitches.

4 *Next row* (WS) Knit through back loop of each stitch. Work 4-row repeat of Drop-stitch pattern to desired length less second border (scarf shown has 51 repeats). Knit 1 row. Do not turn work.

Chart A

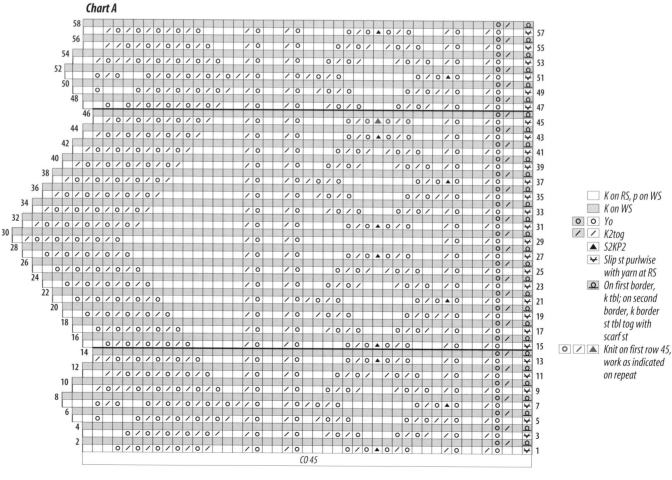

K on RS, p on WS
K on WS
○ Yo
╱ K2tog
▲ S2KP2
⎁ Slip st purlwise with yarn at RS
⧀ On first border, k tbl; on second border, k border st tbl tog with scarf st
○ ╱ ▲ Knit on first row 45, work as indicated on repeat

Second border

5 Slip first stitch from needle onto crochet
   hook and crochet cast on 45 stitches—92
   stitches on needle (47 scarf stitches, 45
   border stitches). Work as First border from
   * to **, working Chart A as knitted-on
   border. Bind off.

Block piece to measurements.

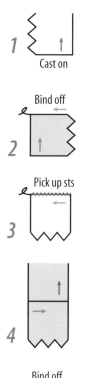

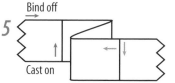 BOOKS

93

Holly Berries
with fir cone lace border from *Weldon's*, 1895

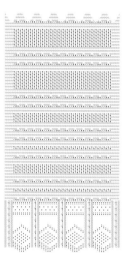

10" x 80"

10cm/4"

34 [grid]
24

• over stockinette stitch
(knit on RS, purl on WS)

1 2 3 4 5 6

• *Super Fine weight*
700 yds

Straight or circular
3.25mm/US 3, or size to obtain
gauge

&

• stitch markers
• blunt needle
• crochet hook for cast-on

Shown in JAGGERSPUN Zephyr
1 tube in 3161 Real Red
Alternate yarn:
LORNA'S LACES Helen's Lace

Notes

1 See *Techniques,* page 166, for crochet cast-on, knitted-on border (including Single Join), and blocking. **2** Match the tension of the bind-off to the cast-on edge.

First border

1 Crochet cast on 32 stitches. * Knit 1 row.
Work 26-row repeat of Chart A four times, Rows 1–7 once. **
2 Bind off, placing the last stitch on a holder.

Center of scarf

3 Turn work and pick up slip stitches along straight edge of border, then return stitch from holder to needle, for a total of 56 stitches.
4 **Next row** (WS) Knit through back loop of each stitch. Knit 4 rows.
Work Rows 1–46 of Chart B once, then Rows 13–34.
Work 28-row repeat of Chart C nine times.
Work Chart B, Rows 13–34, then Rows 1–44. Do not turn work.

Second border

5 Slip first stitch from needle onto crochet hook and crochet cast on 32 stitches—88 stitches on needle (56 scarf stitches, 32 border stitches). Work as First border from * to **, working Chart A as knitted-on border. Bind off.
Block piece to measurements.

1 Cast on

2 Bind off

3 Pick up sts

4 [diagram with arrows]

5 Bind off / Cast on

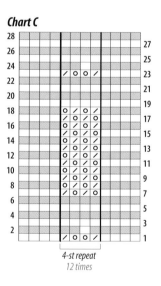

Chart B

4-st repeat
12 times

Chart C

4-st repeat
12 times

□ K on RS, p on WS
▨ K on WS, p on RS
○ Yo
╱ K2tog
● Make berry; see instructions
⤵ Slip st purlwise with yarn at RS
Ω On first border, k tbl;
on the second border, k border st tbl tog with 1 scarf st
Ω On first border, k2tog tbl;
on the second border, k2border sts tbl tog with 1 scarf st

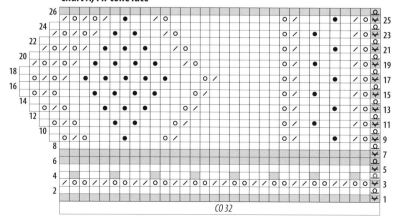

Chart A, Fir cone lace

CO 32

MAKE BERRY

Knit into front, back, front, back, front of a stitch—5 stitches on needle.

[Slip these 5 stitches to left needle . . .

. . . and knit] once, . . .

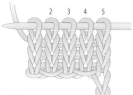

. . . twice, . . .

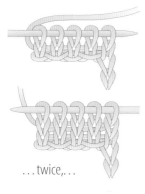

. . . three times, . . .

Pass 2nd, 3rd, 4th, and 5th stitches one at a time, over first stitch.

Scarf

with French trellis border from *Weldon's* 1890 and bramble leaf center

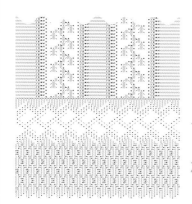

12" x 62"

10cm/4"

38

20

• over garter stitch
(knit all rows)

1 **2** 3 4 5 6

• Fine weight
450 yds

Straight or circular
4.5mm/US 7, or size to obtain gauge

&

• stitch markers
• blunt needle
• crochet hook for cast-on

Shown in hand-spun silk
Alternate yarns: FIESTA La Luz or
HABU 2/10 Kusaki-Zome

Notes

1 See *Techniques*, page 166, for crochet cast-on, SSK, SK2P, knitted-on border (including Single Join), and blocking. *2* Match the tension of the bind-off to the cast-on edge.

First border

1 Crochet cast on 51 stitches. * Purl 1 row.
Work 16-row repeat of Chart A eight times. Knit 1 row .**
2 Bind off, placing the last stitch on a holder.

Center of scarf

3 Turn work and pick up slip stitches along straight edge of border, then return stitch from holder to needle, for a total of 66 stitches.
4 ***Next row*** (WS) Knit through back loop of each stitch.
Work 10-row repeat of Chart B sixteen times, or to desired length less second border.
Knit 1 row. Do not turn work.

Second border

5 Slip first stitch from needle onto crochet hook and crochet cast on 51 stitches—117 stitches on needle (66 scarf stitches, 51 border stitches). Work as First border from * to **, working Chart A as knitted-on border. Bind off.

Block piece to measurements.

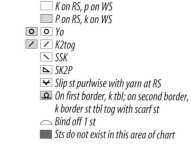

	K on RS, p on WS
	P on RS, k on WS
O	Yo
/	K2tog
\	SSK
⊿	SK2P
⊻	Slip st purlwise with yarn at RS
Ω	On first border, k tbl; on second border, k border st tbl tog with scarf st
⌒	Bind off 1 st
■	Sts do not exist in this area of chart

Chart A, French trellis border

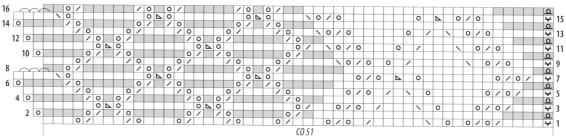

CO 51

Chart B, Bramble leaf insertion

28 - st repeat
2 times

1
Cast on

2
Bind off

3
Pick up sts

4

5
Bind off
Cast on

Scarf

with edging 21 and insertion 25 from *The Knitted Lace Pattern Book*, Thompson Bros., Kilmarnock, Scotland, 1850

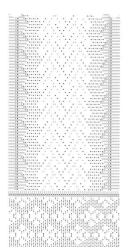

11"x 71"

10cm/4"

26 **18**

• over stockinette stitch
(knit on RS, purl on WS)

1 2 **3** 4 5 6

• Light weight
550 yds

Straight or circular
5mm/US 8, or size to obtain gauge

• stitch markers
• blunt needle
• crochet hook for cast-on

Shown in hand-dyed silk
Alternate yarns:
COLINETTE Tao, FIESTA La Luz, or
SKACEL Seta Bella

Notes

1 See *Techniques*, page 166, for crochet cast-on, SK2P, knitted-on border (including Single Join), and blocking. **2** Match the tension of the bind-off to the cast-on edge.

First border

1 Crochet cast on 41 stitches. * Purl 1 row. Work 28-row repeat of Chart A four times. Knit 1 row. **

2 Bind off, placing the last stitch on a holder.

Center of scarf

3 Turn work and pick up slip stitches along straight edge of border, then return stitch from holder to

needle, for a total of 58 stitches.

4 **Next row** (WS) Knit through back loop of each stitch. Work 12-row repeat of Chart B 21 times, or to desired length less second border. Knit 1 row. Do not turn work.

Second border

5 Slip first stitch from needle onto crochet hook and crochet cast on 41 stitches—99 stitches on needle (58 scarf stitches, 41 border stitches). Work as First border from * to **, working Chart A as knitted-on border. Bind off.

Block piece to measurements.

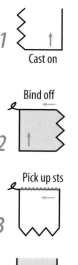

1 Cast on

2 Bind off

3 Pick up sts

4

5 Bind off

Cast on

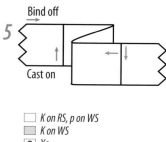

☐ K on RS, p on WS
▨ K on WS
○ Yo
╱ K2tog
◸ SK2P
⤳ Slip st purlwise with yarn at RS
 On first border, k tbl; on second border, k border st tbl tog with scarf st

Chart A, Border

CO 41

Chart B, Center pattern

58-st panel

Double-bordered scarf
with diamond borders adapted from *Weldon's*, 1904

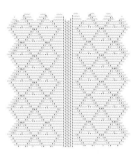

17" x 66"

10cm/4"

32 ▦ **18**

• over garter stitch (knit all rows)

1 **2** 3 4 5 6

• Fine weight
475 yds

Straight or circular needles
4.5mm/US 7, or size to
obtain gauge

4mm/G

&

• stitch markers
• blunt needle

NEEDFUL/LANA GATTO
Mohair Royal 2 balls in 3135

NOTES
1 See *Techniques*, page 166, for crochet cast-on, SK2P, and blocking.
2 Match tension of the bind-off to the cast-on edge.

SCARF
Crochet cast on 58 stitches (25 for each border + 8 for center).
Next row Knit 25, place marker (pm), knit 8, pm, knit to end.
Next row Knit 25, slip marker (sm), work Row 1 of Chart A over next 8 stitches, sm, work Row 1 of Chart B over next 25 stitches.
Next row Work Row 2 of Chart B, sm, work Row 2 of Chart A, sm, work Row 1 of Chart B. Continue to work patterns as established, following Pattern Row Sequence diagram, for a total of twenty 20-row repeats of Pattern Row Sequence, or to desired length.

Note Double-bordered scarves require careful attention. Mark the right side of the work, and keep track of each pattern row as it is worked to avoid confusion. A hint: you work an even row of Chart B as you approach the center of the scarf and an odd row as you approach the edge.
Knit 2 rows and bind off loosely to match cast-on tension.

Optional finish Work single crochet or crochet picot edging along cast-on and bind-off edges.
Crochet picot edging
Work chain 4 (ch 4) and 1 single crochet (1 sc) in first stitch, * 1 sc in next stitch; 1 sc, ch 4, 1 sc in next stitch; repeat from * to last stitch, end 1 sc, ch 4.

Block piece to measurement.

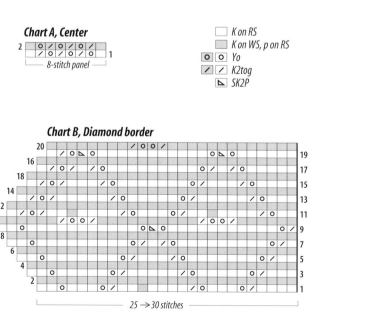

Chart A, Center

8-stitch panel

☐ K on RS
▨ K on WS, p on RS
o Yo
╱ K2tog
◣ SK2P

Chart B, Diamond border

25 → 30 stitches

PATTERN ROW SEQUENCE

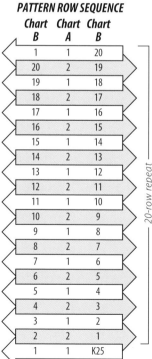

Chart B	Chart A	Chart B
1	1	20
20	2	19
19	1	18
18	2	17
17	1	16
16	2	15
15	1	14
14	2	13
13	1	12
12	2	11
11	1	10
10	2	9
9	1	8
8	2	7
7	1	6
6	2	5
5	1	4
4	2	3
3	1	2
2	2	1
1	1	K25

20-row repeat

Dolphin lace

from *Weldon's* 1887, with an insertion of Miss Lambert's center pattern for a Shetland scarf, 1845

EXPERIENCED LACE

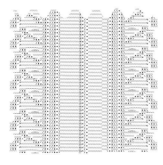

12" x 57"

10cm/4"

38

20

• over garter stitch
(knit all rows)

1 **2** 3 4 5 6

• Fine weight
650 yds

4.5mm/US 7, or size
to obtain gauge

4mm/G

&

• stitch markers
• blunt needle

Shown in hand-dyed 2-ply silk
Alternate yarns:
HABU 2/10 Kusaki-Zome or
almost any Fine weight yarn

NOTES

1 See *Techniques,* page 166, for crochet cast-on and blocking.
2 Match tension of the bind-off to the cast-on edge.

Crochet picot edging

Work chain 4 (ch 4) and 1 single crochet (1 sc) in first stitch, * 1 sc in next stitch; 1 sc, ch 4, 1 sc in next stitch; repeat from * to last stitch, end 1 sc, ch 4.

DOUBLE-BORDERED SCARF

Crochet cast on 60 stitches (20 for each border + 20 for insertion).
Next row [Knit 20, place marker (pm)] 2 times, knit to end.

Next row Knit 20, slip marker (sm), work Row 1 of Chart A over next 20 stitches, sm, work Row 1 of Chart B over next 20 stitches.

Next row Work Row 2 of Chart B, sm, work Row 2 of Chart A, sm, work Row 1 of Chart B. Continue to work patterns as established, following Pattern Row Sequence diagram, for a total of twenty-eight 12-row repeats of Pattern Row Sequence, or to desired length.
Note Double-bordered scarves require careful attention. Mark the right side of the work, and keep track of each pattern row as it is worked to avoid confusion. A hint: you work an even row of border chart (B) as you approach the center of the scarf and an odd row as you approach the edge.

Knit 2 rows and bind off loosely to match cast-on tension. Do not cut yarn.

Finish with single crochet or crochet picot edging along cast-on and bind-off edges.
Block piece to measurement.

PATTERN ROW SEQUENCE

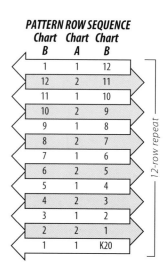

Chart A, Center pattern

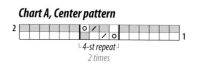

Chart B, Dolphin lace

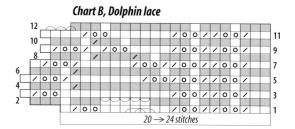

☐ K on RS, p on WS
▨ P on RS, k on WS
◯ Yo
╱ K2tog
⌢ Bind off 1 st
⌣ Cast on 1 st
Dolphin st, Row 1

DOLPHIN STITCH

On first row,

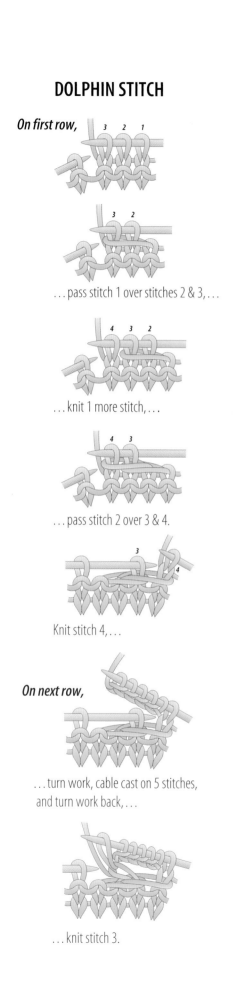

… pass stitch 1 over stitches 2 & 3, …

… knit 1 more stitch, …

… pass stitch 2 over 3 & 4.

Knit stitch 4, …

On next row,

… turn work, cable cast on 5 stitches, and turn work back, …

… knit stitch 3.

Weldon's Practical Knitter

Weldon's Practical Needlework first appeared in 1886 as a monthly collection of instructions for all kinds of needlework. Each issue concentrated on a particular branch of needlework such as knitting, crochet, tatting, or embroidery.

Volume 1, Series 1, How to Knit Useful Garments begins, perhaps surprisingly, with a kind of refresher course on knitting. It gives insufficient information for a complete novice, so was possibly aimed at women who had been taught the rudiments as children, and not knitted since that time. There is a half-square shawl in Spotted Knitting (see page 124) and another shawl in Open Diamond pattern (similar to diamonds on pages 34 and 59). Both shawls have simple borders to be sewn on. Other patterns such as slippers, baby booties and combinations, mittens, gentleman's vest, child's drawers and vest combined, all appear to be aimed at the family's needs for warmth and comfort.

The second Issue in 1886, *How to Knit 38 Useful Articles for Ladies, Gentlemen and Children*, was mainly an extension of the first, with the addition of a ball knitted like an orange. Probably not as frivolous as it sounds, for children at that time had few luxuries.

Also, several multipurpose patterns were given for everything from curtains to tray cloths. Inaccuracy was common, giving the impression that some patterns may not have been knitted before going to print. On a knitted shawl with center diamonds and border (see page 18), the border instructions "pick up stitches all round the shawl using four pins, and extra stitches around the corners for fullness," would be sufficient to discourage many knitters now accustomed to circular needles. The pinnacle of this issue was a Knitted round Shawl on four bone knitting needles (see page 28). There was no illustration, but this turned out to be a real piece of history. Also Clarence Border and Diamond Insertion (see page 82) hinted that more elaborate lace patterns were just around the corner.

The 1st Series of 1887 offers 39 Useful Articles, another refresher on knitting in which it describes a revival of the "lost arts," and a quote from Chatterton,

> *She sayde as her whytte hondes white hosen were knyttinge,*
> *Whatte pleasure ytt ys to be married.*

Knitting hints from early issues include two ways to hold the yarn: German (in left hand) and English (in right hand, the most common method); and slipping a stitch at the beginning of row for neatness.

Terminology develops: knitting on two needles is called *flat web* and is used mostly for edgings, though some articles are knit this way. To decrease is *narrow*, to increase is *widen*, a *turn* is 2 rows, to *rib* is to work alternate rows of plain (knit) and purl. But technique is still simple: only k2tog and k3tog are used; no directional decreases at this early stage.

By 1889 several patterns have names such as Maltese, Dutch, Venetian, Canadian. These may relate to fashion and increasing world contact rather than their actual origins. Beaded cuffs in *knitting silk*, and lace edging for underlinen bring a touch of luxury to Victorian austerity. Instructions for a *respirator* can only tempt the imagination.

Volume 5, 1890, *How to Knit Edgings, Borders, Veils, Shawls &c., with Fifé lace yarns* is the beginning of fine lace knitting with borders and small lace patterns for design-it-yourself projects, as well as some complete shawl patterns. Most patterns had names either from nature or with royal and travel connections. Again, many patterns contained inaccuracies, some quite serious, but it was in this Series (Nos. 12–15) that I found the basis of a number of projects. After all that had been available previously, it was a treasure house. Beautiful wide borders, many of which had originally been intended for household items, had new potential as the focus of scarves or beautiful large shawls, and two cotton *D'Oyleys* knitted on four steel needles could well have been a beginner's introduction to circular knitting.

Weldon's Practical Knitter

Fashion changed. *Volume 10*, 1895, brought yet more very wide borders, with textured rather than lacy patterns using knit/purl, cable, bobbles, bells, ruffles, and geometric designs. A hexagon knitted with four long needles is fairly challenging. Knitters were being stretched as each month's new issue arrived.

From 1900 (*Volume 47*) to around the time of Queen Victoria's death in 1901, instructions were given to miter corners of shawl and quilt borders. These were not always successful, especially the earlier ones which had to be sewn together. At this stage the concept of knitted-on borders had not been realized, and miters were an attempt to avoid bunching at the corners when sewing-on borders.

It is remarkable that one of the last patterns in this series was for a cake doily with an eight-pointed star and trellis. This was yet another version of the Baby's Cap in Jane Gaugain's first book (see page 26). Also Wide Blackberry lace (see page 124) had made a come-back. The chrysalis of 1886 had become a butterfly.

In the course of 28 years, Victorian knitting had developed into a beautiful art form. Despite its increasing sophistication, the old patterns had never lost favor, but they had developed, often by extension and incorporation into larger patterns. Many of the wide borders can be broken down into at least two basic patterns. Most have as their basis either the Vandyke edging of Gaugain and Lambert, or the sloped edging of Mrs. Hope. All originate in the basic version given by Miss Watts in 1837 (see page 4).

A complete list of Weldon's publications can be found in
The History of Knitting–Richard Rutt, p 242, 136
Batsford, London, 1987; many as hard-cover reprints from
Interweave Press.

This has to be one of the prettiest and most romantic shawls I have ever knitted.

The original pattern, comprised of ten panels of shell pattern with a separately knitted border, suggested "...4 oz of best soft white merino wool and two bone knitting needles No.10 (3.25mm)...." I worked twelve panels, in a mohair/silk blend with larger needles, but the size could be adjusted easily with different needles, yarn, or by reducing or increasing the number of panels knitted. Since every other row is purled, it grows quickly.

Lady's circular cape
in shell pattern

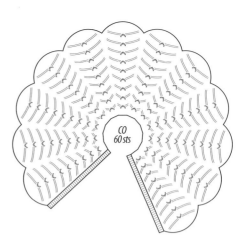

1 Cast on and work center of cape.

INTERMEDIATE LACE

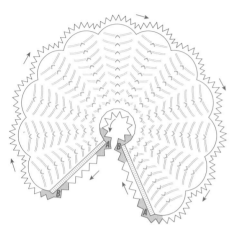

Radius 23"

10cm/4"

26 **:::**

18

• over stockinette stitch
(knit on RS, purl on WS)

1 **2** 3 4 5 6

• *Fine weight*
1100 yds

4.5mm/US 7, or size to obtain gauge,
80cm (32") or longer

Two 4mm/US 6

&

• stitch markers
• blunt needle
• small amount smooth yarn for
cast-on

ROWAN Kidsilk Haze
5 balls in 590 Pearl

Notes

1 See *Techniques*, page 166, for lace cast-ons, knitted-on border (including Single Join and Double Join), grafting, and blocking. *2* If necessary, change to longer circular needles as number of stitches increases.

Corner A

Work 6 Double Joins (DJ) before corner—2 repeats of Chart B. Work 4 DJ, 4 Single Joins (SJ)—2 repeats of chart B.

Corner B

Work 4 SJ, 4 DJ before corner—2 repeats of Chart B. Work 6 DJ—2 repeats of Chart B.

CAPE CENTER

1 Using a lace cast-on, cast on 60 stitches. Work Rows 1–81 of Chart A—684 stitches. Do not bind off. Leave stitches on circular needle.

BORDER

2 ***Work knitted-on border*** Using a lace cast-on, cast on 16 stitches onto double-pointed needle (dpn).
Beginning at center back, * work 12-row repeat of Chart B, working 6 Single Joins for each repeat and ending 6 stitches before corner.

3 Work Corner A.

4 Work Single Joins, ending 8 rows before next corner.

5 Work Corner B.
Continue working Chart B, working Single Joins into live stitches along bottom edge, work Corner A, work Single Joins along other front edge, work Corner B, work to center back. Place loops from border cast-on edge onto free dpn. Cut yarn and graft ends together.

BLOCK

Block to a circle with a 46" diameter as follows: first pin cast-on row into circle with front borders overlapping, then block cape and neck border out from neck circle. Be certain each repeat of the scallop pattern lies in a straight line from neck to lower edge.

2 Knitted-on border Lace cast on and work Single Joins to 6 stitches from corner.

3 Work Corner A.

4 Work Single Joins to 8 rows before bottom corner.

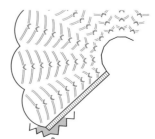

5 Work Corner B. Continue to work knitted-on border along bottom edge, Corner A, front edge, Corner B, and to center back. Graft ends together.

Chart A, Cape

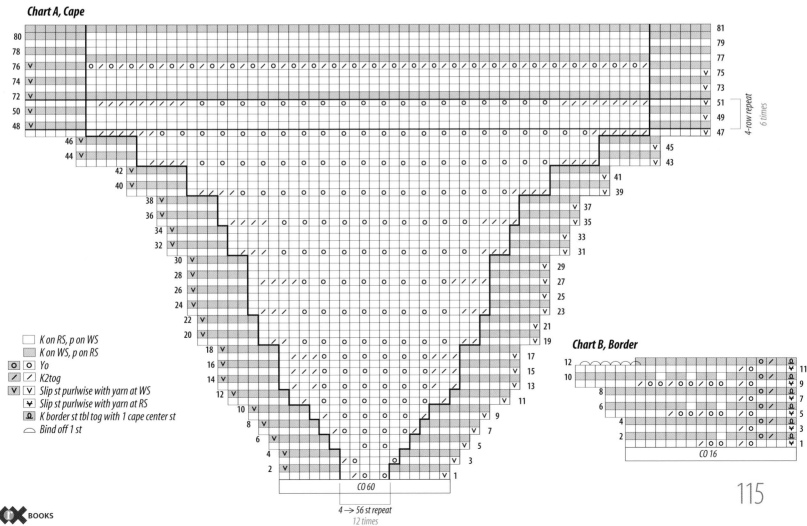

Key:
- ☐ K on RS, p on WS
- ▨ K on WS, p on RS
- ○ Yo
- ╱ K2tog
- V Slip st purlwise with yarn at WS
- ⩔ Slip st purlwise with yarn at RS
- ⍟ K border st tbl tog with 1 cape center st
- ⌢ Bind off 1 st

Chart B, Border

CO 16

CO 60

4 → 56 st repeat
12 times

4-row repeat
6 times

XX BOOKS

The Harebell fichu was inspired by Lace collars which were so fashionable during the Victorian period. The 'Pellerine' (1820's) was a wide collar which extended to the top of the shoulders, and this later extended to a cape—the preferred garment to wear with a wide skirt. What began as decoration, ended as a garment. Around 1880, Cromwell collars, named after the collars worn by Oliver Cromwell and the English Puritans who emigrated to America, became fashionable. Many were deeply pointed in front, others square front and back.

In order to display this pretty Harebell lace pattern, the fichu is begun on a shaped neckband, with the lace knitted-on sideways, like a shawl border.

A harebell fichu

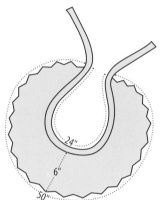

10cm/4"
46
24
• over garter stitch
(knit all rows)

1 2 3 4 5 6
• Super Fine weight
300 yds

3.25mm/US 3, or size to get
gauge, 60cm (24") or longer

• stitch markers
• blunt needle

JADE SAPPHIRE Lacey Lamb
1 ball in 407 Seafoam

Picot edge
Cast on 2 stitches, bind off 2 stitches.

Double Join Work 3 rows of Chart B. At the end of the 4th row, k3tog: the last stitch of lace with the slip-stitch loop from two lace rows below and the next neckband stitch.

Double Make One (M1) Join Work 3 rows of Chart B. At the end of the 4th row, k3tog: the last stitch of lace with slip stitch loop from two lace rows below and a M1 before the next neckband stitch. No neckband stitch knitted-off on this row.

Single Join Work 1 row of Chart B. At the end of the 2nd row, k2tog: the last stitch of lace with the next neckband.

Note
See *Techniques*, page 166, for k3tog, SSK, SK2P, SK3P, SK4P, M1, knitted-on border, grafting, and blocking.

Neckband
Cast on 209 stitches and place markers at the *'s as follows:
40 stitches * 20 stitches * 7 stitches * 21 stitches * 33 stitches * 21 stitches * 7 stitches * 20 stitches * 40 stitches.
Next 4 rows Work picot edge, knit to end.
Shape neckband
Next 12 rows Work picot edge, knit to 4th marker, work Chart A on center 33 stitches, knit to end.
Knit one more row, turn, and bind off 40 stitches. Remove marker, purl 20 stitches and remove marker, turn. Use these 20 stitches as if cast-on stitches and work Chart B, Row 1.
Note In order to shape the fichu and avoid holes, stitches are knitted off the neckband at different rates as Single Joins, Double Joins, and Double M1 Joins. A pencil and paper is helpful to record rows.

Attaching Harebell lace to neckband
Next 7 stitches of neckband Work [1 Double Join, 1 Double M1 Join] 7 times, ending with Row 2—3 repeats + 2 rows.
Next 21 stitches of neckband Work 8 Double Joins, 1 Single Join, and [1 Double Join, 1 Single Join] 6 times ending with Row 18—4 repeats of chart.
Center 69 stitches of neckband Work 2 Single Joins, 66 Double Joins and 1 Single Join—15 repeats; 22 repeats total.
Next 21 stitches of neckband Work [1 Single Join, 1 Double Join] 6 times, 1 Single Join, 8 Double Joins, ending with Row 16—4 repeats.
Next 7 stitches of neckband Work [1 Double M1 Join, 1 Double Join] 7 times, ending with Row 18—3 repeats; 29 repeats total.

Break off yarn, leaving a 30" length. Thread a darning needle and graft the next 20 stitches of neckband to the 20 stitches of Harebell lace. Rejoin yarn to last 40 stitches and bind off loosely.

Block piece to measurements.

Chart A

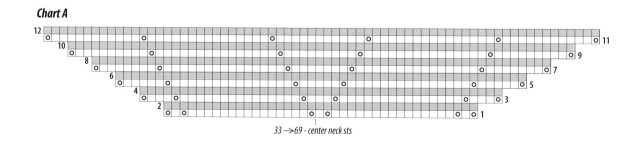

33 → 69 - center neck sts

Chart B, Harebell Lace

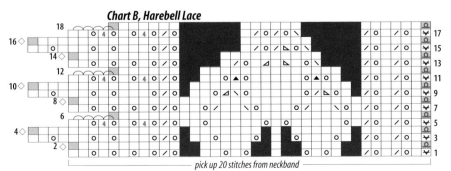

pick up 20 stitches from neckband

☐	K on RS, p on WS
▨	K on WS, p on RS
o	Yo
╱	K2tog
╲	SSK
◺	SK2P
◿	K3tog
▲	SK3P
4	SK4P
⥥	Slip st purlwise with yarn at RS
⚮	Join as per instructions.
⌒	Bind off 1 st
◇	Picot. Cast on 2 sts, bind off 2 sts
■	Sts do not exist in these areas of chart

Throughout the Victorian period, fichus were worn over dresses to cover the front and back of the bodice, for warmth, modesty, or decoration. Their shape and size varied according to fashion. Some came to a point at the back; others were rounded like a cape, with ends crossed at the waist and tied with a bow, or fastened with a button at the chest. In 1881 *The Girl's Own Paper* says, "Fichus are used more and more, and serve to turn a morning dress into a useful and becoming one for evening wear without much expense, and with very little trouble."

The opera fichu

INTERMEDIATE LACE

Center panel measures
40" x 3", border is 3" deep

10cm/4"

40 · over garter stitch
(knit all rows)
using 3.25mm/US 3 needles

24

1 2 3 4 5 6

· Super Fine weight
700 yds

Straight or circular
2.25mm/US 1 and 3.25mm/US 3,
or size to obtain gauge

3.75mm/US 5, 80cm (32") or longer

&

· stitch markers
· blunt needle
· small amount of smooth yarn
for cast-on

JADE SAPPHIRE Lacey Lamb
1 ball in 214 Melon

Note

See *Techniques*, page 166, for lace cast-ons, SSK, and blocking.

1 **CENTER PANEL**

Using a lace cast-on and 3.25mm/US 3 needle, cast on 245 stitches.
Next row (WS) Slip 1 purlwise with yarn at WS (sl 1), k2tog, knit to end—244 stitches.
Knit 7 rows. Work 14-row repeat of Chart A 2 times. Knit 2 rows, changing to largest, circular
needle before working last row.

BORDER

2 Pick up and knit 20 stitches along side of center panel, knit 244 from cast-on edge, and pick
up and knit 20 stitches along second side—528 stitches.

3 Place marker and join. Knit 1 round. *Next round* * Yo, k1; repeat from * to end—1056
stitches. *Next round* Knit. Work 2-round repeat of Chart B 10 times.
Bind off using picot bind-off: * cast on 2 stitches, bind off 5 stitches; repeat from * to end.
Block border Thread a strong cotton cord through each picot, stretch edges to fullest width,
then cut cord, leaving about 18 inches at each end. Tie a knot. Wash. Pin out center first. Gently
pull cord to shape border and pin at 3-inch intervals. Remove center pins and leave to dry.

NECKBAND AND TIES

4 With WS of Border facing and 2.25mm/US 1 needle, pick up 240 center stitches from outer
row of center panel (top edge). *Next row* (WS) Knit. *Next row* * K1, k2tog; repeat from * to
end—160 stitches.

5 *Ties and neck shaping, Row 1* Knit 46, place marker (pm), knit 68, pm, knit 46, cable cast on 55
stitches—215 stitches. *Row 2* Knit to end, cable cast on 55 stitches—270 stitches.

6 *Row 3* Picot (cast on 2 stitches, bind off 2 stitches), knit to marker, [k2tog, k1, k2tog, knit
16] 3 times, k2tog, k1, k2tog, knit to end—262 stitches. *Row 4* Picot, knit to end, removing
markers. *Next 4 rows* Picot, knit to end. Bind off, being careful not to bind off 55 stitches of
ties too tightly.

Block piece lightly; it should remain quite springy.

	K on RS, p on WS
▨	K on WS
○	Yo
╱	K2tog
╲	SSK
☑ ☑	Slip st purlwise with yarn at WS

Chart A, Center panel

12-st repeat
20 times

Chart B, Miss Lambert's lace pattern

6-st repeat
176 times

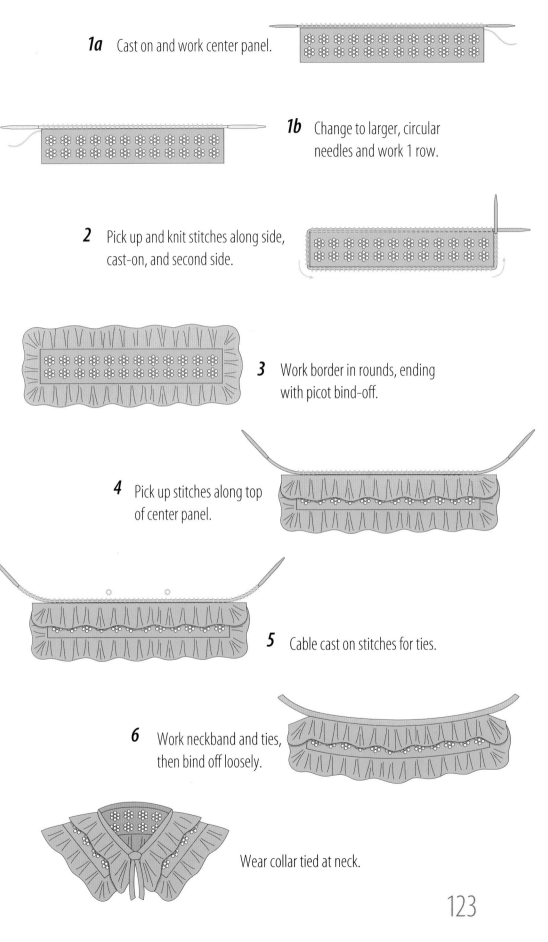

1a Cast on and work center panel.

1b Change to larger, circular needles and work 1 row.

2 Pick up and knit stitches along side, cast-on, and second side.

3 Work border in rounds, ending with picot bind-off.

4 Pick up stitches along top of center panel.

5 Cable cast on stitches for ties.

6 Work neckband and ties, then bind off loosely.

Wear collar tied at neck.

123

A half-square shawl was published in *Weldon's Practical Knitter, Vol. 1. No.1, Series 4,* 1886, under the heading, 'How to knit useful garments.' The border pattern is simple, quick to knit, and was originally sewn onto the triangle, but I recommend that it be knitted on for neatness.

The author mentions that Spotted Knitting is also called "Trinity Stitch… from it being composed of three stitches in one." The repetition of "Father, Son, and Holy Ghost" was intended to keep the knitter's mind focused in the right direction.

Half-square
in Trinity stitch

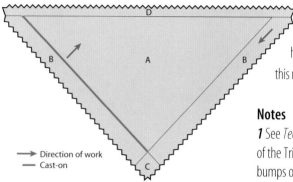

42" x 75"

10cm/4"

28

20

• over stockinette stitch
(knit on RS, purl on WS)

1 **2** 3 4 5 6

• Fine weight
1250 yds

4mm/US 6, or size to obtain gauge,
60cm (24") or longer

Two 4mm/US 6

&

• stitch markers
• blunt needle

Shown in handspun polwarth/kid
Alternate yarns: TWISTED SISTERS
Petite Voodoo

→ Direction of work
— Cast-on

This shawl was published twice, in 1886 as a triangle and in 1904 as a square with a truly magnificent border, so I decided to use the triangle of 1886 with the wide border of 1904. However, the border was not intended for a half square, so I reduced it on the hypotenuse from 28 stitches to 7 stitches, for better balance and fit. The later pattern was printed "in response to several enquiries," so this must have been popular.

Notes
1 See *Techniques*, page 166, for lace cast-ons, knitted-on border (including Single Join and Double Join), and blocking. *2* The bump of the Trinity stitch pops out on the reverse side, which becomes the right side of the shawl. Be careful to match bumps of center with bumps of wide border.

SHAWL
Cast on 242 stitches.
Work Chart A, Rows 1–8—238 stitches.
Repeat Rows 5–8, working 1 fewer 4-stitch repeat every 4-row repeat, until 10 stitches remain.
End as shown in last 5 rows of Chart A. Fasten off.

BORDER
Work knitted-on border Using a lace cast-on, cast on 28 stitches onto double-pointed needle (dpn). Place shawl center with bumps up to begin joining border to side stitches on even rows of border.
Work Chart B, set-up row, knitting last stitch of border together with last edge stitch of shawl.
Continue working Chart B as a knitted-on border: On even-numbered rows, knit last border stitch together with an edge stitch of shawl, ending with first edge stitch. Two rows of border attach to two rows of center triangle.
Work Chart C, mitering the corner with short rows and knitting last stitch of Row 48 together with a cast-on stitch of shawl.
Work Chart B, knitting last even-rowed stitch of border together with 2 cast-on stitches of shawl, ending with Row 7 of chart. Two rows of border attach to two cast-on stitches. Be certain that the second side has the same number of pattern repeats as the first side.
Next row Without breaking the yarn, bind off 6 stitches, knit 6, turn.
Work Chart D as knitted-on border On even-numbered rows, knit last border stitch together with a wide border stitch to edge of triangle, then with a shawl stitch between each Trinity stitch (every 4 rows of hypotenuse) to cast-on for wide border, then with a cast-on border stitch. End with Row 8 of chart.

Block piece to measurements.

Trinity stitch
After Row 3 of Chart A.

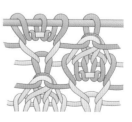

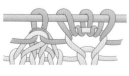

On Row 5, the p3tog is worked on top of the KPK from Row 3, and the KPK is worked on top of the p3tog.

Chart A, Center triangle

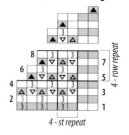

4 - st repeat

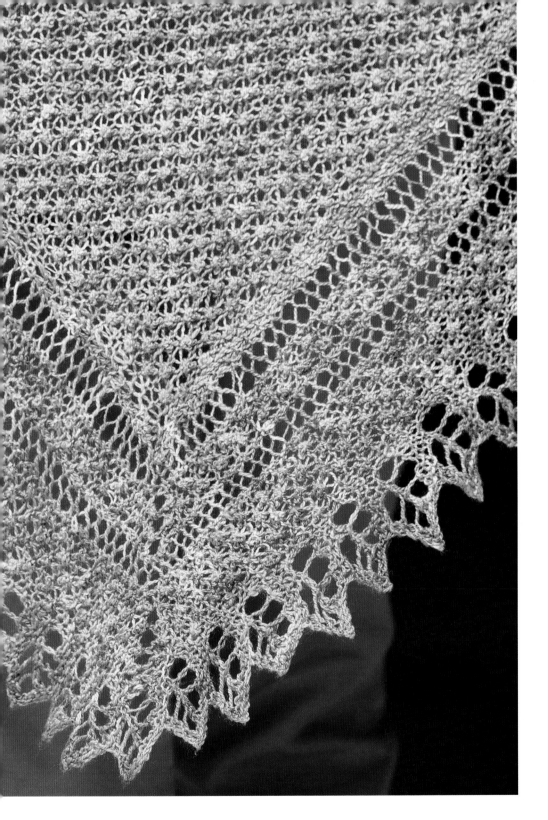

Chart C, Wide border corner

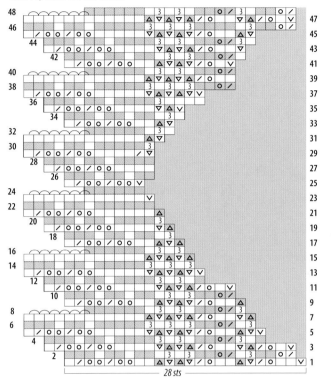

28 sts

Legend:

☐	K on odd rows, p on even rows
▨	K on even rows, p on odd rows
3	P3
3	Sl 1, p2
3	K3
O	Yo
/	K2tog
△	P3tog
▲	P4tog
▽	K1, p1, k1 in same st
V	Slip st purlwise with yarn at WS
ⱱ	Slip st purlwise with yarn at RS
⚲	K border st tbl tog with 1 center panel st per instructions
▨	Sts left unworked during short-row shaping
⌒	Bind off 1 st

Chart B, Wide border for straight edging

set-up

CO 28

Chart D, Border for hypotenuse

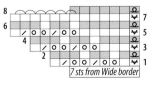

7 sts from Wide border

Understanding lace

Joining the edging to one out of every 4 rows of shawl along the hypotenuse helps avoid stretching of the bias fabric.

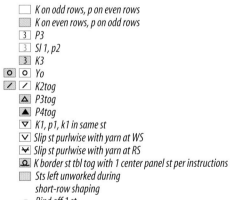

The Victorian British Empire reached to every corner of the globe, and constantly brought new novelties into the country, developing a thirst for the exotic. The Crimean war of 1854 brought an Oriental influence in sympathy with Britain's ally. Women began to sport rich Turkish-style fabrics and colors, and tasselled trims were popular. Foreign names were given to knitting patterns—this Syrian shawl, for example. The royal family's intercontinental links also contributed to the thirst for far-off countries—Queen Victoria's godfather was Tsar Nicholas I, her beloved Prince Albert was Prince of Saxe-Coburg, and her eldest daughter, Princess Victoria Adelaide Mary Louise, married Friedrich III, German Emperor and King of Prussia.

Shoulder shawl
in Syrian pattern

EASY LACE

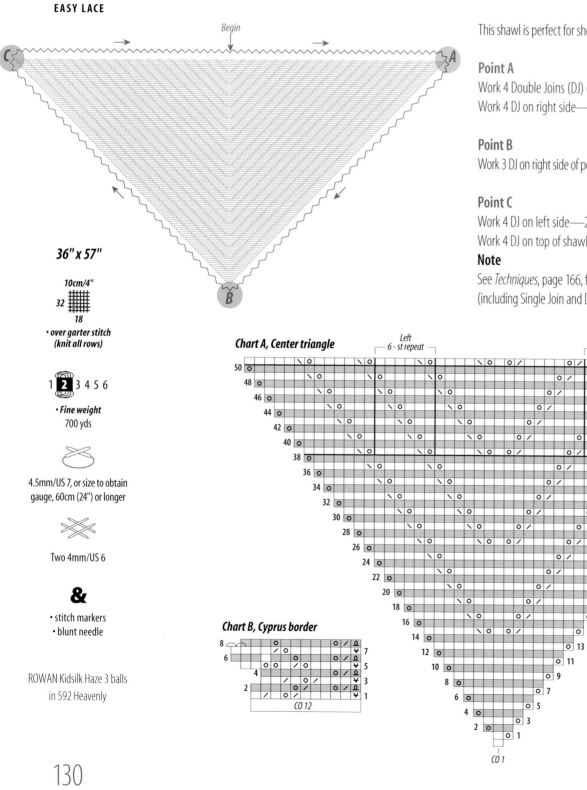

Begin

36" x 57"

10cm/4"

32 / 18

• over garter stitch (knit all rows)

1 **2** 3 4 5 6

• *Fine weight*
700 yds

4.5mm/US 7, or size to obtain gauge, 60cm (24") or longer

Two 4mm/US 6

&

• stitch markers
• blunt needle

ROWAN Kidsilk Haze 3 balls in 592 Heavenly

This shawl is perfect for showing off a fluffy, textured, or painted yarn.

Point A
Work 4 Double Joins (DJ) on top of shawl—2 repeats of Chart B.
Work 4 DJ on right side—2 repeats of Chart B.

Point B
Work 3 DJ on right side of point, 3 DJ on left side of point—3 repeats of Chart B.

Point C
Work 4 DJ on left side—2 repeats of chart B.
Work 4 DJ on top of shawl—2 repeats of Chart B.

Note
See *Techniques*, page 166, for lace cast-ons, SSK, SK2P, M1, knitted-on border (including Single Join and Double Join), grafting, and blocking.

Chart A, Center triangle

Left 6 - st repeat

Right 6 - st repeat

12 - row repeat

Chart B, Cyprus border

CO 12

CO 1

☐ K on RS, p on WS
▧ P on RS, k on WS
⊙ Yo
╱ K2tog
╲ SSK
⌄ Slip st purlwise with yarn at RS
⚳ K border st tbl tog with 1 center triangle st

CENTER TRIANGLE

Cast on 1 stitch onto circular needle. Work Chart A, Rows 1–50—51 stitches.

Note Every 12-row repeat begins and ends the same; the only difference is the number of 6-stitch repeats. Every 12 rows, 12 stitches are increased, adding one additional repeat to each side of triangle.

Continue working thus for a total of 18 yarn-over stripes, ending with Row 50—231 stitches. Leave stitches on needle. Cut yarn.

BORDER

Note Place the left half of shawl stitches on a holder before beginning the border.

Work knitted-on border Using a lace cast-on, cast on 12 stitches onto double-pointed needle (dpn). Beginning at center back stitch, work 8-row repeat of Chart B 28 times, working 4 Single Joins for each repeat. Continue working Chart B, joining border to center triangle as follows: Work Point A. * [Work 4 Single Joins—1 repeat of Chart B] 27 times. ** Work Point B. Repeat between * and **. Work Point C. Transfer top stitches onto needle, marking 1 stitch near center. Work 8-row repeat of Chart B 28 times, ending at center. Pick up stitches from border cast-on edge on free dpn. Cut yarn and graft ends together.

Block piece to measurements.

Historic note

Originally described in *Weldon's Volume 6, Issue 62*, 1891, as "a simple yet effective pattern for a three cornered shoulder shawl to be knitted with either Shetland wool on No. 11 needles [3mm], or with Fifé lace yarn on No. 9 needles [3.75mm]," this shawl also appeared in *No. 152*, 1898. It would have originally been finished with a knotted fringe, but I suggest bordering it with the Cyprus edging from the 1890 issue of *Weldon's How to Knit Borders*.

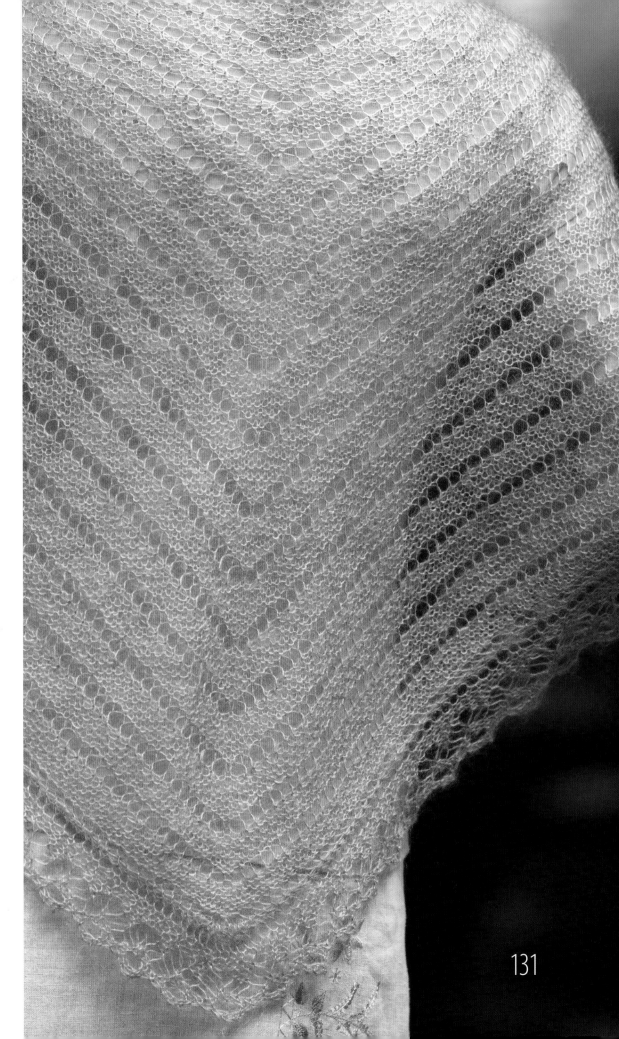

I have worked this pattern in several different yarns, from fine silk to Shetland wool to a 4-ply kid mohair-merino blend; all are pleasing. The shawl is worked from the point upwards to the hypotenuse, with the border knitted on afterwards. To make it larger, just knit more repeats!

Shoulder shawl
in cherry leaf pattern

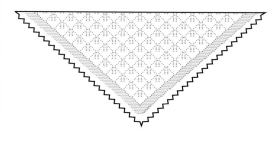

33" x 75"

10cm/4"

28

20

• over stockinette stitch
(knit on RS, purl on WS)

1 **2** 3 4 5 6

• Fine weight
900 yds

4.5mm/US 7, or size to obtain
gauge, 60cm (24") or longer

Two 4mm/US 6

&

• stitch markers
• blunt needle

Shown in handspun silk
Alternate yarns: FIESTA La Luz or
HABU 2/10 Kusaki-Zome
Almost any Fine or Light weight
yarn will work; with a thicker
yarn, use larger needles and work
fewer repeats.

Note
See *Techniques*, page 166, for crochet cast-on, SSK,
SK2P, M1, knitted-on border, and blocking.

CENTER TRIANGLE
Cast on 3 stitches onto circular needle. Work Chart A,
Rows 1–44.

Note Every 10-row repeat begins and ends the same;
the only difference is the number of 12-stitch repeats
worked. Every 10 rows, 12 stitches are increased, adding
one additional repeat.

Continue working thus for a total of fifteen 10-row
repeats—207 stitches.

Knit 14 rows. Bind off loosely.

Using crochet cast-on, cast on 11 stitces onto double-
pointed needle.

*Work Chart B as knitted-on border along diagonal
edges of center triangle* On even-numbered rows, knit
last border stitch through back loop (tbl) together with a
center triangle stitch EXCEPT at point. At point, on every
other even-numbered row knit the last border stitch
together with a triangle stitch 7 times. Bind off.

Work along straight edge of shawl and ends of border
with crochet picot edging:

Row 1 (RS) Single crochet (sc) in each st at edge of knitting.

Row 2 * Ch 3, sc into next sc, sc; repeat from *, ending
ch 3, sc.

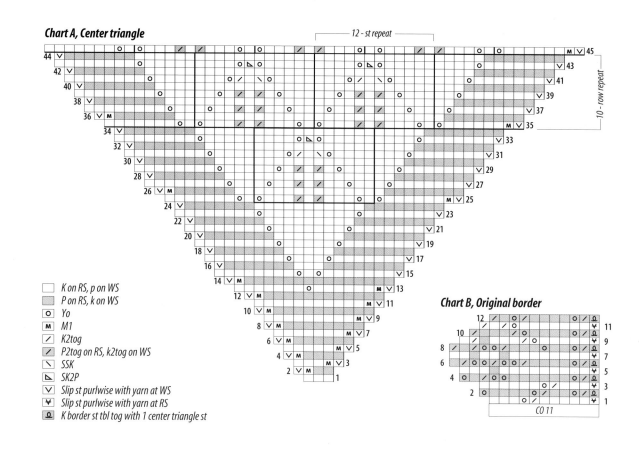

Chart A, Center triangle

12 - st repeat

10 - row repeat

□ K on RS, p on WS
▨ P on RS, k on WS
○ Yo
Ⓜ M1
╱ K2tog
▨ P2tog on RS, k2tog on WS
╲ SSK
◪ SK2P
⋁ Slip st purlwise with yarn at WS
⋎ Slip st purlwise with yarn at RS
Ω K border st tbl tog with 1 center triangle st

Chart B, Original border

CO 11

Historic note

The original description in *Weldon's Practical Knitter, Vol. 6*, 1891 is as follows: "Our engraving represents the corner of a half square shoulder shawl worked in a new and elegant pattern. Shetland wool and a pair of long steel knitting needles, No.12 [2.75mm] were employed for the model, which is very light and lacy, but if a heavier shawl is desired, a medium-sized yarn and No.9 [3.75mm] needles may be used." As a matter of interest, this pattern was repeated in *Vol.20, No.233, Series 62*, 1905.

This light and lacy pattern begins with the full number of stitches at the edge of the scalloped border then stitches are decreased gradually in the course of working through the clover leaf lace, the insertion, and the central pattern, until a triangular piece of knitting is accomplished, ending in the center of the hypotenuse. A square shawl may be made by knitting four pattern repeats instead of two.

Three-cornered shawl
in clover pattern

33" x 68"
40" x 82"

10cm/4"
34/28
24/20
• over stockinette stitch
(knit on RS, purl on WS)

1 2 3 4 5 6

•Super Fine weight
• 1300 yds
• 2200 yds

3.25mm/US 3/3.75mm/US 5, or
size to obtain gauge, 80–60cm
(32–24") change to shorter needle
as stitch number decreases

&
• stitch markers
• blunt needle

JADE SAPPHIRE Lacey Lamb
2 balls in 407 Seafoam
Shown in gray handspun
Alternate yarn: KARABELLA Super
Cashmere Fine

Notes

1 See *Techniques*, page 166, for loop cast-on, yo, SSK, SK2P, knitted-on border, and blocking. **2** Begin and end each row of shawl with 2 stockinette stitches. These stitches are not included in charts or stitch counts. **3** Stitch counts in the pattern are given for one section of shawl only.

SHAWL

Using loop cast-on, cast on 624 stitches: 2 stitches for each edge and 310 for each half of shawl (multiple of 13 + 11). Place marker after 312 stitches. Work chart patterns as follows: work 2 stockinette stitches (edge stitches); work row of chart once (to center marker); work row of chart again; end shawl row by working 2 stockinette stitches (edge stitches).

Work Chart A, Rows 1–4—308 stitches.
Work Chart B, Rows 1–8—277 stitches.
Work Chart C, Rows 1–26 beginning with 21 pattern repeats—251 stitches, 19 repeats.
Work Chart C, Rows 3–26—227 stitches, 17 repeats.
Work Chart C, Rows 3–24—209 stitches.
Work Chart D, Rows 1–2—175 stitches.
Work Chart E, Rows 1–28—149 stitches.
Work Chart F until 13 stitches remain. End as shown at top of Chart F. Fasten off.

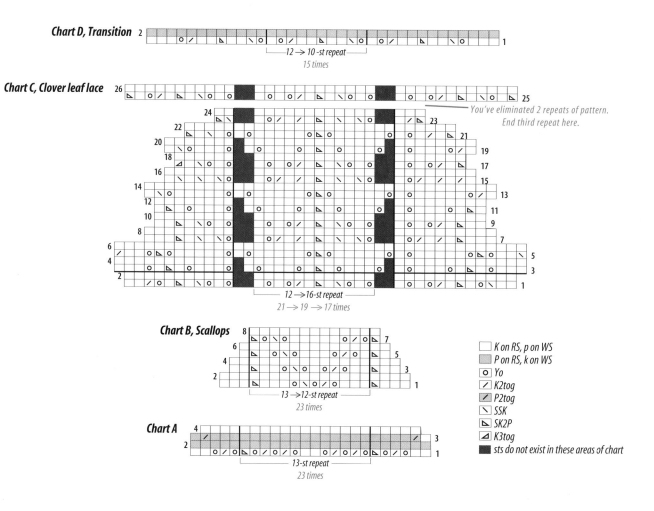

Chart D, Transition
12 → 10 -st repeat
15 times

Chart C, Clover leaf lace
You've eliminated 2 repeats of pattern.
End third repeat here.
12 →16-st repeat
21 → 19 → 17 times

Chart B, Scallops
13 →12-st repeat
23 times

Chart A
13-st repeat
23 times

□ K on RS, p on WS
▨ P on RS, k on WS
○ Yo
╱ K2tog
◪ P2tog
╲ SSK
◣ SK2P
◿ K3tog
■ sts do not exist in these areas of chart

Chart F, Clover pattern for center

16
14
12
10
8
6
4
2
16 · 15
14 · 13
12 · 11
10 · 9
8 · 7
6 · 5
4 · 3
2 · 1

⌐ 8-st repeat ¬
16 times

Chart E, Eyelets & open holes

28 · 27
26 · 25
24 · 23
22 · 21
20 · 19
18 · 17
16 · 15
14 · 13
12 · 11
10 · 9
8 · 7
6 · 5
4 · 3
2 · 1

⌐ 4-st repeat ¬
36 times

Chart G, Willow border

8 · 7
6 · 5
4 · 3
2 · 1

CO 12

BORDER

Pick up 268 stitches along the longest side of the shawl (hypotenuse).
Cast on 12 stitches and work Chart G as a knitted-on border. On even-
numbered rows, knit first border stitch together with a shawl stitch.
Block shawl upwards from the center point to the hypotenuse.

The original of this piece was gossamer, worked in finest Fifé lace yarn with number 15 steel needles—about 1.5mm or US000!

Myrtle leaf shawl
with willow border

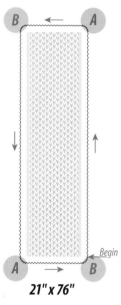

INTERMEDIATE LACE

21" x 76"

10cm/4"

28

20

• over stockinette stitch
(knit on RS, purl on WS)

 1 2 3 4 5 6

• Super Fine weight
950 yds

3.75mm/US 5, or size to obtain
gauge, 60cm (24") or longer

Two 3.75mm/US 5

 &

• stitch markers
• blunt needle

Shown in handspun Hebridean
Alternate yarns: KARABELLA
Light-weight Cashmere or MISTI
ALPACA Lace

Corner A

Work 2 Single Joins (SJ), 1 Double Join (DJ)—1 repeat of Chart B.
Work 2 DJ two times—2 repeats of Chart B.
Work 1 DJ on long side and 1 DJ on short side—1 repeat of Chart B.
Work 2 DJ two times—2 repeats of Chart B.

Corner B

Work 2 DJ two times—2 repeats of Chart B.
Work 1 DJ on short side, 1 DJ on long side—1 repeat of Chart B.
Work 2 DJ two times—2 repeats of Chart B.
Work 1 DJ, 2 SJ—1 repeat of Chart B.

Notes

1 See *Techniques*, page 166, for lace cast-ons, SSK, SSP, knitted-on border (including Single Join and Double Join), grafting, and blocking.
2 Chart B, Willow border, joins at the end of RS rows, not at the end of WS rows as in most shawls.
3 Keep tension tight when working yo's and the k2tog at the top of the leaves in rows 7 and 13 of Chart A.

CENTER PANEL

Using a lace cast-on, cast on 87 stitches onto circular needle (multiple of 11 + 10).

Next row Slip 1, knit 2 together, knit to the end of the row—86 stitches.
Next 3 rows Slip 1, knit to the end of the row.
Work Chart A, Row 1.
Work Chart A, Rows 2–13 forty times, placing marker at beginning of Row 13 in first repeat.
Next 4 rows Slip 1, knit to the end of the row.
Leave stitches on circular needle. Cut yarn.

BORDER

Work knitted-on border Using a lace cast-on, cast on 12 stitches onto double-pointed needle (dpn).
Beginning at marked slip stitch at right edge of center panel, * work 8-row repeat of Chart B 57 times, working 4 Single Joins for each repeat. Continue working Chart B, joining border to center panel as follows: Work Corner A. [Work 4 Single Joins—1 repeat of Chart B] 19 times. Work Corner B. Repeat from *, placing 86 loops from cast-on edge onto circular needle before starting Corner A.
Pick up loops from border cast-on edge onto free dpn. Cut yarn and graft ends together.

Block piece to measurements.

Chart A, Myrtle leaf pattern

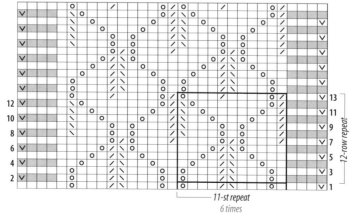

12-row repeat

11-st repeat
6 times

Chart B, Willow border

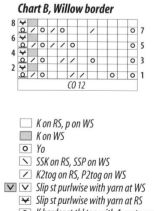

CO 12

☐ K on RS, p on WS
▨ K on WS
○ Yo
╲ SSK on RS, SSP on WS
╱ K2tog on RS, P2tog on WS
V̌ Slip st purlwise with yarn at WS
Y̌ Slip st purlwise with yarn at RS
Q K border st tbl tog with 1 center panel st

Understanding Lace

Chart B may seem unorthodox since it is the only border in this book which is joined to the center panel at the end of right-side rows. But in 1890, there was no knitting orthodoxy.

Weldon's original instructions suggested either "a charming light wrap" in fine lace yarn, or a more substantial garment in a thicker yarn. The center pattern was so pretty that I almost decided not to add the border, but in the end could not resist the temptation. However, a scarf in just the melon pattern would be lovely, say six pattern repeats with four garter stitches at each side and six rows at each end.

Melon pattern
for a shawl or scarf

17" x 72"

10cm/4"

26

18

• over stockinette stitch
(knit on RS, purl on WS)

1 **2** 3 4 5 6

• Fine weight
700 yds

4.5mm/US 7, or size to obtain
gauge, 60cm (24") or longer

Two 4mm/US 6

&

• stitch markers
• blunt needle
• small amount of smooth yarn
for cast-on

ROWAN Kidsilk Haze
3 balls in 597 Jelly

CORNER A

Work 2 Single Joins (SJ), 1 Double Join (DJ)—1 repeat of Chart B.
Work 2 DJ—1 repeat of Chart B.
Work 1 DJ on long side, 1 DJ on short side—1 repeat of Chart B.
Work 2 DJ—1 repeat of Chart B.

CORNER B

Work 2 DJ—1 repeat of Chart B.
Work 1 DJ on short side, 1 DJ on long side—1 repeat of Chart B.
Work 2 DJ—1 repeat of Chart B.
Work 1 DJ, 2 SJ—1 repeat of Chart B.

Notes

1 See *Techniques*, page 166, for lace cast-ons, knitted-on border (including Single Join and Double Join), grafting, and blocking. **2** The decrease in the first row of the Center Panel reduces the stitch count to the correct pattern multiple; the extra cast-on stitch provides the correct number of loops for the knitted-on border.

Chart A, Melon pattern

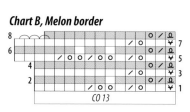

10-st repeat
6 times

Chart B, Melon border

CO 13

CENTER PANEL

Using a lace cast-on, cast on 71 stitches onto circular needle (multiple of 10 + 1).
Work 6-row repeat of Chart A, marking last stitch of Row 1 in third repeat and working chart a total of 62 times—70 stitches. Work Chart A, Rows 1—4.
Leave stitches on circular needle. Cut yarn.

BORDER

Work knitted-on border Using a lace cast-on, cast on 13 stitches onto double-pointed needle (dpn).
Beginning at marked slip stitch at left edge of center panel, * work 8-row repeat of Chart B 44 times, working 4 Single Joins for each repeat. Continue working Chart B, joining border to center panel as follows: Work Corner A. [Work 4 Single Joins—1 repeat of Chart B] 16 times. Work Corner B. Repeat from *, placing 70 loops from cast-on edge onto circular needle before starting Corner A.
Pick up loops from border cast-on edge on free dpn. Cut yarn and graft ends together.

Block piece to measurements.

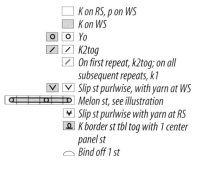

□ K on RS, p on WS
▦ K on WS
○ Yo
╱ K2tog
╱ On first repeat, k2tog; on all
subsequent repeats, k1
∨ Slip st purlwise, with yarn at WS
⊶ Melon st, see illustration
⩔ Slip st purlwise with yarn at RS
Ω K border st tbl tog with 1 center
panel st
⌒ Bind off 1 st

MELON STITCH

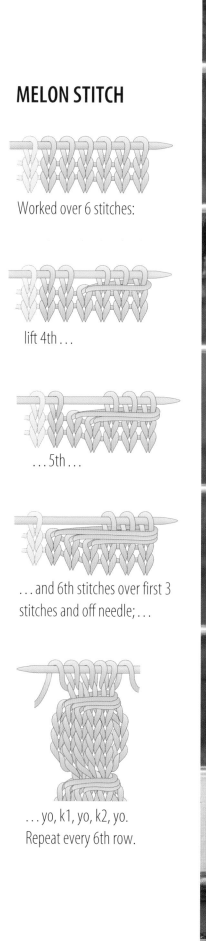

Worked over 6 stitches:

lift 4th . . .

. . . 5th . . .

. . . and 6th stitches over first 3 stitches and off needle; . . .

. . . yo, k1, yo, k2, yo. Repeat every 6th row.

Diamonds and triangles

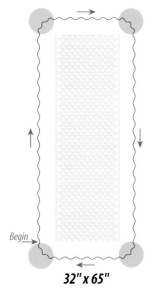

32" x 65"

10cm/4"
26
18
• over stockinette stitch
(knit on RS, purl on WS)

1 **2** 3 4 5 6

• Fine weight
1300 yds

4.5mm/US 7, or size to obtain
gauge, 60cm (24") or longer

Two 4mm/US 6

&
• stitch markers
• blunt needle
• small amount of smooth yarn
for cast-on

NEEDFUL/LANA GATTO
Mohair Royal
5 balls in 3135

CORNER

Work 1 Single Join (SJ), 4 Double Joins (DJ), 1 Triple Join (TJ)—1 repeat
of chart.
Work 2 TJ on this side, 2 TJ on next side—1 repeat of chart.
Work 1 TJ, 4 DJ, 1 SJ—1 repeat of chart.

NOTE

See *Techniques*, page 166, for lace cast-ons, SSK, SK2P, knitted-on border (including Single, Double, and Triple Joins), grafting, and blocking.

CENTER PANEL

Using lace cast-on, cast on 89 stitches (multiple of 8 + 17) onto
circular needle. Knit 3 rows.
Next row (WS) Knit, decreasing 4 stitches across row (by k2tog)—
85 stitches.
Work 12-row repeat Chart A thirty-two times, marking last stitch of
first row of second repeat.

Next row Knit, increasing 3 stitches across row—88 stitches. Knit 3
rows. Leave stitches on circular needle. Cut yarn.

BORDER

Work knitted-on border Using a lace cast-on, cast on 32 stitches
onto double-pointed needle (dpn).
Beginning at marker at left edge of center panel, * work 24-row
repeat of Chart B 15 times, working 12 Single Joins for each repeat.
Continue working Chart B, joining border to center panel as follows:
Work Corner. [Work 12 Single Joins—1 repeat of chart] 6 times.
Work Corner. Repeat from *, placing 88 loops from cast-on edge onto
circular needle before starting next Corner.
Pick up loops from border cast-on edge on free dpn. Cut yarn and
graft ends together.

Block piece to measurements.

Chart A, Diamonds and triangles

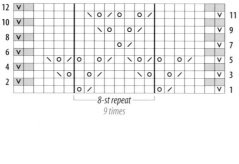

8-st repeat
9 times

K on RS, p on WS
K on WS
Yo
K2tog on RS, p2tog on WS
P2tog on RS, k2tog on WS
SSK
SK2P
Slip st purlwise with yarn at WS
Slip st purlwise with yarn at RS
K border st tbl tog with 1 center panel st

Chart B, Border

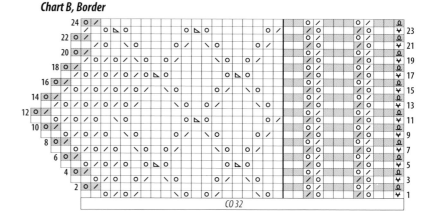

CO 32

The big, beautiful, and simple border of the shawl in Queen's Imperial Wool from the 1904 issue caught my eye. Alas, as I have found with many of these old patterns, the center oak leaf pattern was mathematically unworkable. Despite swatching and graphing, and with no illustrations as a guide, I could not arrive at anything remotely knittable.

However in *Weldon's* 1888 issue, I found a garter stitch diamond pattern for a shawl with a border. When this diamond pattern was paired with the 1903 border, I decided the two were meant to be together. This shawl is a delight, the pattern is fairly easy to knit and also reversible.

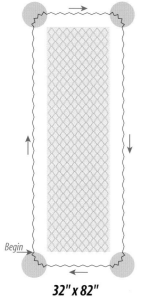

32" x 82"

10cm/4"

32 | 18

• *over garter stitch (knit all rows)*

1 **2** 3 4 5 6

• *Fine weight*
1150 yds

4.5mm/US 7, or size to obtain
gauge, 60cm (24") or longer

Two 4mm/US 6

&

• stitch markers
• blunt needle
• small amount of smooth yarn
for cast-on

NEEDFUL/LANA GATTO
Mohair Royal
5 balls in 10083

The Victoria shawl

CORNER

Work 5 Single Joins (SJ), 2 Double Joins (DJ)—1 repeat of Chart B.
Work 3 DJ, 1 Triple Join (TJ)—1 repeat of Chart B.
Work 1 TJ, 3 DJ—1 repeat of Chart B.
Work 2 DJ, 5 SJ—1 repeat of Chart B.

NOTE

See *Techniques*, page 166, for lace cast-ons, knitted-on border (including
Single Join, Double Join, and Triple Join), SK2P, grafting, and blocking.

CENTER PANEL

Using lace cast-on, cast on 86 stitches (multiple of 10 + 16) onto
circular needle.
Next row Slip 1 purlwise with yarn at WS (sl 1), knit 2 together, knit
to end—85 stitches.
Next row Sl 1, knit to end.
Work 16-row repeat of Chart A 25 times, marking last stitch of Row
4 of second repeat. Knit 2 rows. Leave stitches on circular needle.
Cut yarn.

BORDER

Work knitted-on border Using a lace cast-on, cast on 25 stitches
onto double-pointed needle (dpn).
Beginning at marked slip stitch at left edge of center panel, * work 18-
row repeat of Chart B 20 times, working 9 Single Joins for each repeat.
Continue working Chart B, joining border to center panel as follows:
Work Corner. [Work 9 Single Joins—1 repeat of Chart B] 7 times.
Work corner. Repeat from *, placing 85 loops from cast-on edge onto
circular needle before starting Corner.
Pick up loops from border cast-on edge on free dpn. Cut yarn and graft
ends together.

Block piece to measurements.

□ K on RS
▨ P on RS, k on WS
○ Yo
╱ K2tog
◣ SK2P
∨ Slip st purlwise with yarn at WS
⩔ Slip st purlwise with yarn at RS
Ω K border st tbl tog with 1 center panel st
⌒ Bind off
■ stitches do not exist in these areas of chart

Chart A, Center diamond panel

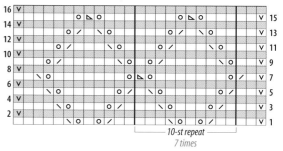

10-st repeat
7 times

Chart B, Border

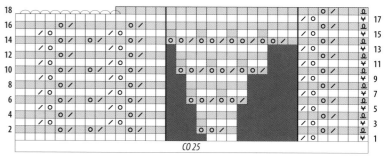

CO 25

Stripes were very fashionable in Victorian England. Even the blinds at Queen Victoria's summer residence on the Isle of Wight had blue and white stripes.

So, it's appropriate that this shawl features panels of open diamond pattern framed by a bold border.

Stripes and torchon lace

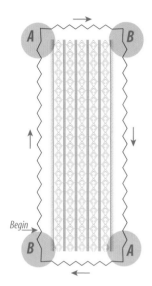

36" x 86"

10cm/4"

26

18

• over stockinette stitch (knit on RS, purl on WS)

1 **2** 3 4 5 6

• Fine weight
• 1350 yds

4.5mm/US 7, or size to obtain gauge, 60cm (24") or longer

Two 4mm/US 6

&

• stitch markers
• small amount of smooth yarn for cast-on

NEEDFUL/LANA GATTO Mohair Royal 6 balls in 2118

CORNER A

Work 1 Single Join (SJ), 8 Double Joins (DJ)—1 repeat of Chart B. Work 3 Triple Joins (TJ) on long side; 2 TJ, 1 DJ on short side—1 repeat of Chart B.

CORNER B

Work 1 DJ, 2 TJ on short side; 3 TJ on long side—1 repeat of Chart B. Work 8 DJ, 1 SJ—1 repeat of Chart B.

NOTE

See *Techniques*, page 166, for lace cast-ons, SSK, SK2P, knitted-on border (including Single, Double, and Triple Joins), grafting, and blocking.

CENTER PANEL

Using a lace cast-on, cast on 92 stitches (multiple of 17 + 7) onto circular needle. *Next row* (RS) K2tog, knit to end—91 stitches. Knit 3 rows. Work 18-row repeat of Chart A 23 times, marking last stitch of Row 3 in second repeat. Knit 4 rows. Leave stitches on circular needle. Cut yarn.

BORDER

Work knitted-on border Using a lace cast-on, cast on 20 stitches onto double-pointed needle (dpn).

Beginning at marked slip stitch at left edge of Center Panel, * work 34-row repeat of Chart B 11 times, working 17 Single Joins for each repeat. Continue working Chart B, joining stitches to center panel as follows: Work Corner A. [Work 17 Single Joins—1 repeat of chart] 5 times. Work Corner B. Repeat from *, placing 91 stitches from cast-on edge onto circular needle before starting Corner A. Place 20 stitches from border cast-on edge on free dpn. Cut yarn and graft ends together.

Block piece to measurement.

Chart A, Open diamond panel

Chart B, Torchon lace border

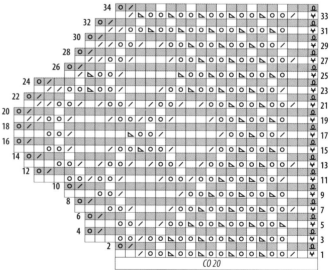

	K on RS, p on WS
	K on WS
o	Yo
/	K2tog
\	SSK
◣	SK2P
V	Slip st purlwise with yarn at WS
ⱴ	Slip st purlwise with yarn at RS
Ω	K border st tbl tog with 1 center panel st

Chart note

Two changes have been made to the open diamond pattern: left slanting decreases have been altered from k2tog to SSK, and the 15-stitch repeat has been extended to 17 stitches in order to give extra faggoting between the diamond stripes.

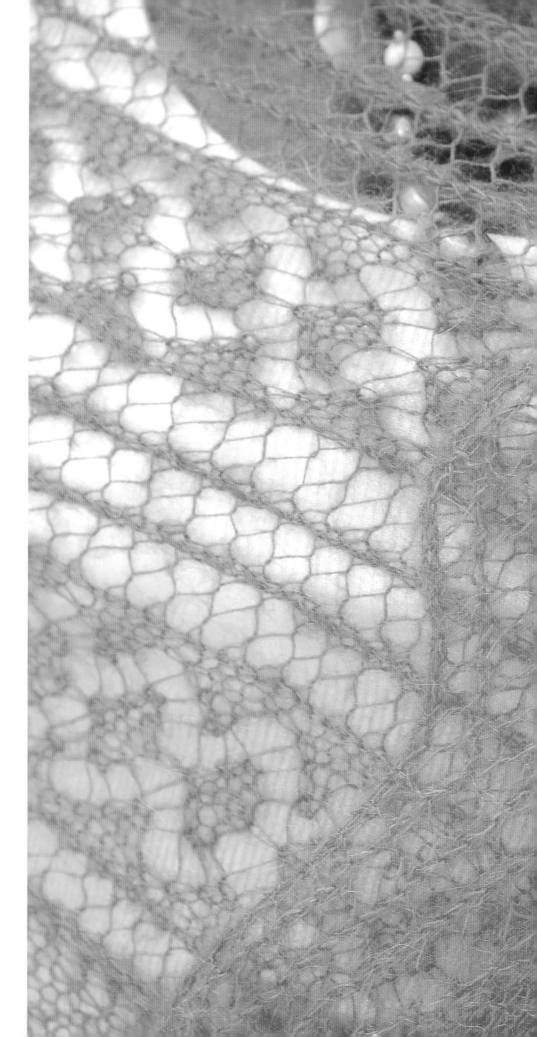

By the 1880's shawls appeared in the vivid new colors made possible by the innovation of aniline dyes.

This shawl's center pattern originally appeared as a Maltese stripe consisting of a series of Maltese crosses. Jane Gaugain's book of 1847 gives a netting pattern for a mitten in Maltese Spotting brought back by Her Majesty Queen Adelaide (Queen Dowager) from her travels in Malta—a favorite destination for wealthy travellers at the time and an island famous for real lace.

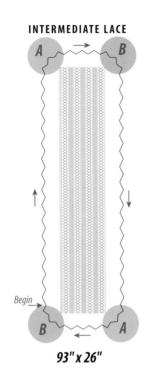

93" x 26"

10cm/4"

26

18

• over stockinette stitch
(knit on RS, purl on WS)

1 **2** 3 4 5 6

• *Fine weight*
1100 yds

• 4.5mm/US 7, or size to obtain
gauge, 60cm (24") or longer

Two 4mm/US 6

&

• stitch markers
• blunt needle
• small amount of smooth yarn
for cast-on

ROWAN Kidsilk Haze 5 balls in
596 Marmalade

The Maltese shawl

CORNER A

Work 5 Single Joins (SJ), 2 Double Joins (DJ), 2 Triple Joins (TJ)—1 repeat of Chart B.
Work 2 TJ, 1 DJ on long side, 1 SJ, 2 TJ on short side—1 repeat of Chart B.
Work 2 DJ, 11 SJ—1 repeat of Chart B.

CORNER B

Work 9 SJ, 3 DJ—1 repeat of Chart A.
Work 2 TJ, 1 SJ on short side, 1 DJ, 2 TJ on long side—1 repeat of Chart A.
Work 2 TJ, 2 DJ, 5 SJ—1 repeat of Chart A.

Notes

1 See *Techniques*, page 166, for lace cast-ons, SSK, SSP, SK2P, knitted-on border (including Single Join, Double Join, and Triple Join), grafting, and blocking. **2** Place markers between repeats of Center panel. **3** Work Center panel first, then work Border, joining stitches to Center panel at end of every WS row.

CENTER PANEL

Using a lace cast-on, cast on 77 stitches onto circular needle.
Next row (WS) P2tog, purl to end of row—76 stitches.
Work 6-row repeat of Chart A, marking last stitch of Row 1 of 45th repeat and working chart a total of 88 times. Knit 1 row. Leave stitches on circular needle. Cut yarn.

BORDER

Work knitted-on border Using lace cast-on, cast on 11 stitches onto double-pointed needle (dpn).
Beginning at marked slip stitch at left edge of Center panel, * work 30-row repeat of Chart B 8 times, working 15 SJ for each repeat. Work Corner A. [Work 15 SJ—1 repeat of Chart B] 3 times. Work Corner B. [Work 15 SJ—1 repeat of Chart B] 8 times. Repeat from *, placing 76 loops from cast-on edge onto circular needle before starting second Corner A. Place loops from cast-on edge onto free dpn. Cut yarn and graft ends together.

Block piece to measurements.

Chart B, Border

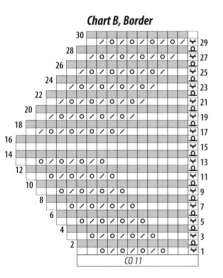

CO 11

Chart A, Center panel

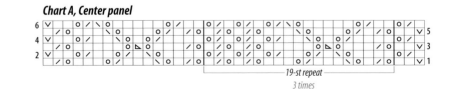

19-st repeat
3 times

	K on RS, p on WS
	K on WS
o	Yarn over
/	K2tog on RS, p2tog on WS
\	SSK on RS, SSP on WS
◣	SK2P
V	Sl st purlwise with yarn at WS
⩔	Sl st purlwise with yarn at RS
⍟	Join as specified

Techniques, Tools, and Talk

TECHNIQUES

LACE CAST-ONS

INVISIBLE CAST-ON

A temporary cast-on
1 Knot working yarn to contrasting waste yarn. Hold needle and knot in right hand. Tension both strands in left hand; separate strands so waste yarn is over index finger, working yarn over thumb. Bring needle between strands and under thumb yarn so working yarn forms a yarn-over in front of waste yarn.

2 Holding both yarns taut, pivot hand toward you, bringing working yarn under and behind waste yarn. Bring needle behind and under working yarn so working yarn forms a yarn-over behind waste yarn.

3 Pivot hand away from you, bringing working yarn under and in front of waste yarn. Bring needle between strands and under working yarn, forming a yarn-over in front of waste yarn. Each yarn-over forms a stitch. Repeat Steps 2–3 for required number of stitches. For an even number, twist working yarn around waste strand before knitting the first row.

CHAIN CAST-ON

A temporary cast-on
1 With crochet hook and waste yarn, loosely chain the number of stitches needed, plus a few extra chains. Cut yarn.

2 With needle and main yarn, pick up and knit 1 stitch into the back 'purl bump' of the first chain. Continue, knitting 1 stitch into each chain until you have the required number of stitches. Do not work into remaining chains.

WASTE-YARN CAST-ON

A temporary cast-on
Cast on with a contrasting waste yarn and knit 4 rows before breaking yarn and changing to main yarn. Unless using mohair, put the stitches on the needle before removing waste yarn.

HISTORIC NOTE *The expression* cast on *was not recorded before 1838, when it appeared in* The Ladies Knitting and Netting Book *by Miss Watts, and was used interchangeably with* put on.

PICKING UP LOOPS FROM A TEMPORARY CAST-ON

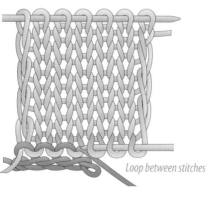

Loop between stitches

Temporary cast-ons use waste yarn to hold the loops that form between stitches under the needle. When this waste yarn is removed, these loops can be placed on a needle and worked into. Use the temporary cast-on of your choice for the center panel and border of shawls with knitted-on borders. Knit the border onto these loops at the bottom of the center panel, and graft the last row of the border to these loops.
Note There is always one fewer loop than cast-on stitches. Adjust for this by casting on one more stitch, then decreasing one in first row; or by simply decreasing in the last row. The instructions in this book include that adjustment.

OTHER CAST-ONS

LOOP CAST-ON (ALSO CALLED E-WRAP CAST-ON)

 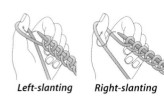 

Left-slanting   *Right-slanting*

1 Hold needle and tail in left hand.
2 Bring right index finger under yarn, pointing toward you.

3 Turn index finger to point away from you.
4 Insert tip of needle under yarn on index finger (see above); remove finger and draw yarn snug, forming a stitch.
Repeat Steps 2–4 until all stitches are on needle.

Loops can be formed over index or thumb and can slant to the left or to the right. On the next row, work through back loop of right-slanting loops

CABLE CAST-ON

1 Start with a slipknot on left needle (first cast-on stitch). Insert right needle into slipknot from front. Wrap yarn over right needle as if to knit.

2 Bring yarn through slipknot, forming a loop on right needle.
3 Insert left needle in loop and slip loop off right needle. One additional stitch cast on.

4 Insert right needle between the last 2 stitches. From this position, knit a stitch and slip it to the left needle as in Step 3.
Repeat Step 4 for each additional stitch.

CIRCLE CAST-ON

Use to cast on a few stitches at center of a flat circle.
1 Holding tail in right hand and yarn in left hand, make a circle.
2 Insert double-pointed needle in circle and draw yarn through, forming a stitch on needle. Do not remove fingers from loop.

3 Bring needle under and then over the yarn, forming a yarn-over on needle.

4 Repeat Steps 2 and 3, ending with Step 2. To cast on an even number, yarn over before beginning the first round.
5 Arrange stitches on 3 or 4 double-pointed needles, pull tail slightly, then begin knitting around, working into the back loops of yarn-overs on the first round. Work several more rounds, then pull tail to close center.

CROCHET CAST-ON

1 Leaving a short tail, make a slipknot on crochet hook. Hold hook in right hand; in left hand, hold knitting needle on top of yarn and behind hook. With hook to left of yarn, bring yarn through loop on hook; yarn goes over top of needle, forming a stitch.

2 Bring yarn under point of needle and hook yarn through loop forming next stitch. Repeat Step 2 until 1 stitch remains to cast on. Slip loop from hook to needle for last stitch.

DARNING IN ENDS

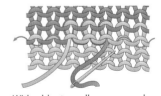

With a blunt needle, weave each yarn through purl bumps for 5–6 stitches: new yarn toward beginning of row, old yarn toward end of row.

ABBREVIATIONS

ch chain

cm centimeter(s)

dec decreas(e)(ed)(es)(ing)

dpn double-pointed needle(s)

g gram(s)

" inch(es)

inc increas(e)(ed)(es)(ing)

k knit(ting)(s)(ted)

LH left-hand

M1 Make one stitch (increase)

m meter(s)

mm millimeter(s)

oz ounce(s)

p purl(ed)(ing)(s) or page

pm place marker

psso pass slipped stitch(es) over

RH right-hand

RS right side(s)

sc single crochet (UK double crochet)

sl slip(ped)(ping)

SKP slip, knit, psso

SSK slip, slip, knit these 2 sts tog

SSP slip, slip, purl these 2 sts tog

st(s) stitch(es)

St st stockinette stitch

tbl through back of loop(s)

tog together

WS wrong side(s)

wyib with yarn in back

wyif with yarn in front

yd(s) yard(s)

yo(2) yarn over (twice) (UK yarn forward)

DECREASES

SSK

1 Slip 2 stitches **separately** to right needle as if to knit.

2 Slip left needle into these 2 stitches from left to right and knit them together: 2 stitches become 1.

The result is a left-slanting decrease.

SKP (SK2P, SK3P, SK4P) sl 1-k1 (k2tog, k3tog, k4tog)-psso

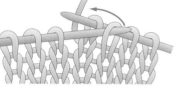

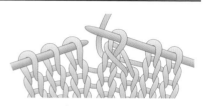

1 Slip 1 stitch knitwise from left needle onto right.

2 Knit 1 (k2tog, k3tog, k4tog) as usual.

3 Pass slipped stitch over knit (ktog) stitch: 2 (3, 4, 5) stitches become 1.

The result is a left-slanting decrease.

SSP

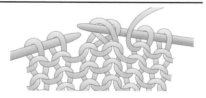

Use instead of p2tog-tbl to avoid twisting the stitches.
1 Slip 2 stitches **separately** to right needle as if to knit.

2 Slip these 2 stitches back onto left needle. Insert right needle through their 'back loops,' into the second stitch and then the first.

3 Purl them together: 2 stitches become 1.

The result is a left-slanting decrease.

S2KP2, sl 2-k1-p2sso

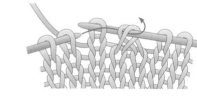

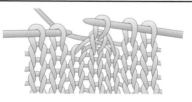

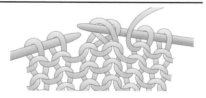

1 Slip 2 stitches **together** to right needle as if to knit.

2 Knit next stitch.

3 Pass 2 slipped stitches over knit stitch and off right needle: 3 stitches become 1; the center stitch is on top.

The result is a centered double decrease.

P2tog ──────────────── K2tog (K3tog) ────────────────

1 Insert right needle into first 2 stitches on left needle.

2 Purl these 2 stitches together as if they were 1. The result is a right-slanting decrease.

1 Insert right needle into first 2 (3) stitches on left needle, beginning with second (third) stitch from end of left needle.

2 Knit these 2 (3) stitches together as if they were 1. The result is a right-slanting decrease.

INCREASES

MAKE 1 LEFT (M1L), KNIT

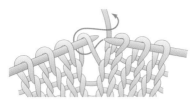

Insert left needle from front to back under strand between last stitch knitted and first stitch on left needle. Knit, twisting strand by working into loop at back of needle.

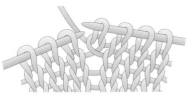

Completed M1L knit: a left-slanting increase.

MAKE 1 RIGHT (M1R), KNIT

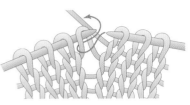

Insert left needle from back to front under strand between last stitch knitted and first stitch on left needle. Knit, twisting the strand by working into loop at front of the needle.

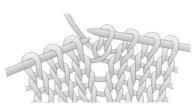

Completed M1R knit: a right-slanting increase.

YARN OVERS

TIPS
- *Check your work carefully as you work the row after a yarn-over row. If you are short a stitch or two, check for missing yarn-overs.*
- *To check for missing yarn-overs in lace patterns that have non-patterned wrong-side rows, try reading the pattern row in reverse to check as you work the next (wrong-side) row.*

YARN OVER (yo)

Between knit stitches
Bring yarn under the needle to the front, take it over the needle to the back and knit the next stitch.

Between purl stitches
With yarn in front of needle, bring it over the needle to the back and to the front again; purl next stitch.

At beginning of a knit row
With yarn in front of needle, knit first stitch.

At beginning of a purl row
With yarn in front of needle, bring it over the needle to the back and to the front again; purl next stitch.

After a knit, before a purl
Bring yarn under the needle to the front, over the needle to the back, then under the needle to the front; purl next stitch.

After a purl, before a knit
With yarn in front of the needle, bring it over the needle to the back; knit next stitch.

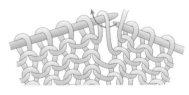

On next row
Purl (or knit) into front of yarn over unless instructed otherwise. The yarn-over makes a hole and adds a stitch.

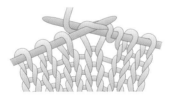

Yarn over twice (yo2)
After bringing yarn over the needle (first yarn-over), wrap yarn completely around needle a second time. On next row, work into double yarn-over as instructed.

PICKING UP A MISSING YARN-OVER

Work to where a yarn-over should be. Insert left needle from front to back under strand between last stitch purled (or knit) and next stitch on left needle. Purl (or knit) into yarn-over.

BASICS

SUSPENDED BIND-OFF

This method makes it very difficult to bind off too tightly.
1 Work (knit or purl) 2 stitches.
2 With left needle, pass first stitch on right needle over second stitch, but leave on left needle.

3 Work next stitch (shown above).
4 Slip both stitches from left needle. Repeat Steps 2–4.

ELONGATED STITCH

1 Knit 1, EXCEPT wrap yarn 2 or more times around needle, instead of once, before drawing new stitch through old stitch.

NOTE
Either a knit or a purl can be elongated.

2 On next row, work the stitch, dropping extra wrap(s) as stitch is pulled off left needle.

SLIP PURLWISE (sl 1 p-wise)

1 Insert right needle into next stitch on left needle from back to front (as if to purl).

2 Slide stitch from left to right needle. Stitch orientation does not change (right leg of stitch loop is at front of needle).

The stitch slipped purlwise can be a knit or a purl.

STRINGING BEADS

Using a loop of thread or fine wire, string required number of beads on yarn.

KNIT THROUGH BACK LOOP (k1 tbl)

1 With right needle behind left needle and right leg of stitch, insert needle into stitch…

2 …and knit.

CHAIN STITCH (ch st, ch)

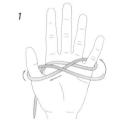

1 Make a slipknot to begin.
2 Catch yarn and draw through loop on hook.

First chain made. Repeat Step 2.

SPLICING YARN

Splicing eliminates the need to darn in ends when joining in a new skein of wool. Separate the plies of the last 3–4" of both the old end and the new skein. Break off (do not cut) half of the plies on each end.

Overlap two ends in one palm. Spit into your other palm and rub your hands together briskly until you can feel heat—about 15 seconds. This join will hold after it is knit into fabric; until then, avoid pulling on it.

WINDING YARN INTO A BALL

1

2

Butterfly wrap

Center-pull ball

For a center-pull ball wrap yarn in figure-8 fashion around fingers 6–8 times (1). Remove wrap from hand. Hold one wing of butterfly between thumb and 2 fingers of left hand; other end of wing stays free. Begin winding yarn around thumb, wing, and fingers. After 10–12 wraps, slip fingers out, but keep thumb in place, turn ball slightly, replace fingers, and wind again. Repeat this process, gradually building a round ball of yarn (2). When finished, tuck end under last set of wraps, and free thumb and fingers. To start knitting, pull butterfly, and yarn will feed from center of ball.

TIP
Some fine yarns, such as a slippery silk, do not behave well in a center-pull ball.

170

GRAFT IN GARTER

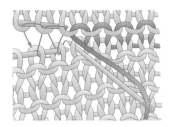

1 Arrange stitches on 2 needles so stitches on lower, or front, needle come out of purl bumps and stitches on the upper, or back, needle come out of smooth knits.

2 Thread a blunt needle with matching yarn (approximately 1" per stitch).

3 Working from right to left, begin with Steps 3a and 3b:
3a Front needle: bring yarn through first stitch *as if to purl,* leave stitch *on needle.*

3b Back needle: repeat Step 3a.

4a Front needle: bring yarn through first stitch *as if to knit, slip off* needle; through next stitch *as if to purl, leave on* needle.

4b Back needle: repeat Step 4a. Repeat Steps 4a and 4b until 1 stitch remains on each needle.

5a Front needle: bring yarn through stitch *as if to knit,* slip *off needle.*

5b Back needle: repeat Step 5a.
6 Adjust tension to match rest of knitting.

TIPS
•When grafting a pattern stitch, practice by tracing the row in your swatch with duplicate stitch in a contrasting color. Then use that as your guide.
•After a little practice, you'll be able to chant as you graft.
For garter stitch, say:
"knit and off,
purl and on," for both front and back needles.
For stockinette stitch, say:
"knit and off, purl and on," for front needle;
"purl and off, knit and on," for back needle.

GRAFT IN STOCKINETTE

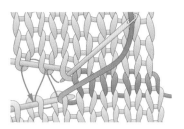

1 Arrange stitches on 2 needles as shown.

2 Thread a blunt needle with matching yarn (approximately 1" per stitch).

3 Working from right to left, with right sides facing you, begin with Steps 3a and 3b:

3a Front needle: bring yarn through first stitch *as if to purl,* leave stitch *on needle.*

3b Back needle: bring yarn through first stitch *as if to knit,* leave stitch *on needle.*

4a Front needle: bring yarn through first stitch *as if to knit, slip off* needle; through next stitch *as if to purl, leave stitch on needle.*

4b Back needle: bring yarn through first stitch *as if to purl, slip off* needle; through next stitch *as if to knit,* leave stitch *on needle.* Repeat Steps 4a and 4b until 1 stitch remains on each needle.

5a Front needle: bring yarn through stitch *as if to knit,* slip *off needle.*

5b Back needle: bring yarn through stitch *as if to purl,* slip *off needle.*

6 Adjust tension to match rest of knitting.

RIPPING BACK: STITCH-BY-STITCH

IN KNIT

 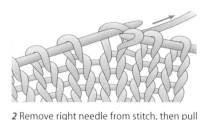

1 Insert left needle into stitch below first stitch on right needle.

2 Remove right needle from stitch, then pull working yarn free.

IN PURL

 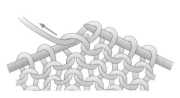

1 Insert left needle into stitch below first stitch on right needle.

2 Remove right needle from stitch, then pull working yarn free.

PICKING UP DROPPED STITCHES

IN KNIT

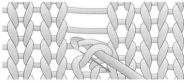

Insert crochet hook into stitch from **front to back** and * bring hook **under** ladder of yarn. Catch yarn and pull through stitch, forming a new stitch on hook. Repeat from * for each ladder. Slip last stitch onto needle.

IN PURL

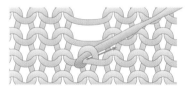

Insert crochet hook into stitch from **back to front** and * bring hook **over** ladder of yarn. Catch yarn and pull through stitch, forming a new stitch on hook. Repeat from * for each ladder. Slip last stitch onto needle.

SINGLE CROCHET (SC)

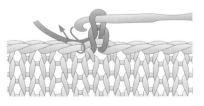 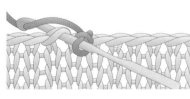 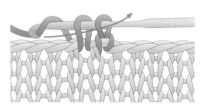

1 Insert hook into a stitch, catch yarn, and pull up a loop. Catch yarn and pull through the loop on the hook.
2 Insert hook into next stitch to the left.

3 Catch yarn and pull through the stitch; 2 loops on hook.

4 Catch yarn and pull through both loops on hook; 1 single crochet completed. Repeat Steps 2–4.

171

Borders are knit onto the center panel of a shawl or scarf in three ways:
• around slipped stitches along both sides of the center panel
• into **open stitches** at the top of the center panel, and
• into **loops between stitches** at bottom of center panel.

The first stitch of odd-numbered border rows are slipped. The last stitch of even-numbered border rows is attached to a slipped stitch, open stitch, or loop of center panel: one join for every 2 rows of border.

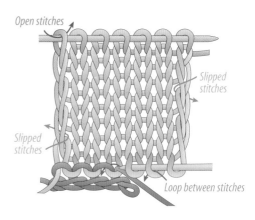

Open stitches

Slipped stitches

Slipped stitches

Loop between stitches

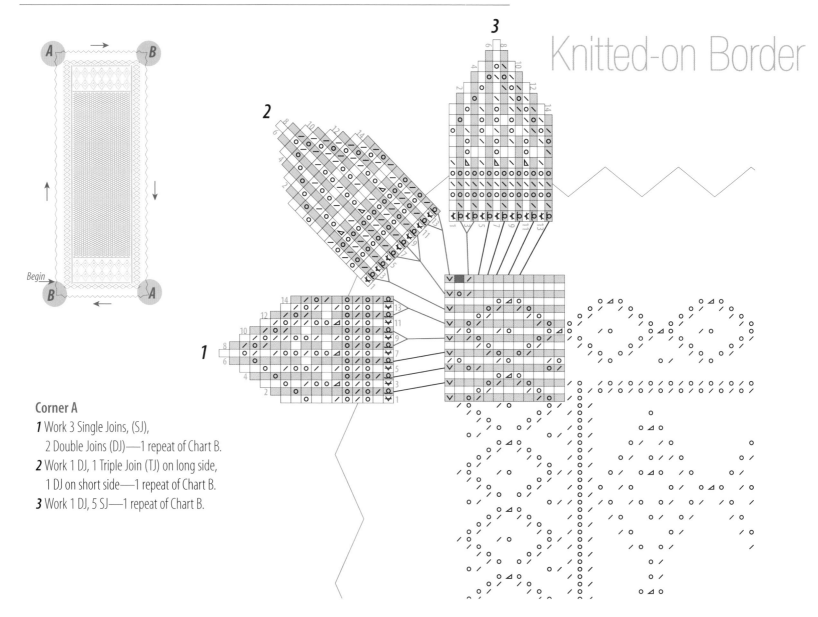

Knitted-on Border

Corner A

1 Work 3 Single Joins, (SJ),
2 Double Joins (DJ)—1 repeat of Chart B.

2 Work 1 DJ, 1 Triple Join (TJ) on long side,
1 DJ on short side—1 repeat of Chart B.

3 Work 1 DJ, 5 SJ—1 repeat of Chart B.

To fit a border to a center panel and ease a border around a corner, three joins are used:

Single Join (SJ) One join to one stitch of center panel: On even-numbered (WS) rows, knit last border stitch through the back loop together with one slipped stitch, top stitch, or bottom loop of center panel. Two border rows joined to one stitch of center panel.

Double Join (DJ) Two joins to one stitch of center panel: Work a Single Join as above; on next WS row, work a second join in the same way and **into the same stitch**. Four border rows joined to one stitch of center panel.

Triple Join (TJ) Three joins to one stitch of center panel: Work a Double Join as above; on next WS row, work a third join in the same way and **into the same stitch**. Six border rows joined to one stitch of center panel.

Begin at the marked stitch along the side of the shawl (it corresponds to the Begin line on the schematic), and work the sequence of Single, Double, and Triple Joins suggested in the project. If you have miscounted and the numbers do not work out perfectly at the corner, it is usually safe to substitute a Double Join for a Single Join, or a Triple Join for a Double Join, to make things fit.

The lace cast-ons provide open loops for this knitting-on process. Note that there is always one fewer loop than cast-on stitches. The instructions in this book adjust for that difference.

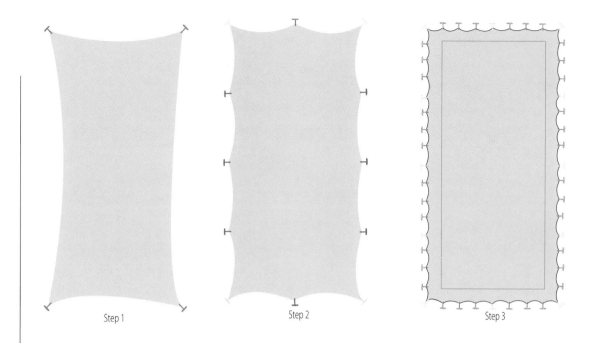

Step 1   Step 2   Step 3

Blocking To Measurements

Wash your swatch or finished lace in warm water (tepid for silk), rinse if required, roll in a towel to remove excess water, and pin out with rust-proof pins.

Pin first
Pin second
Pin third

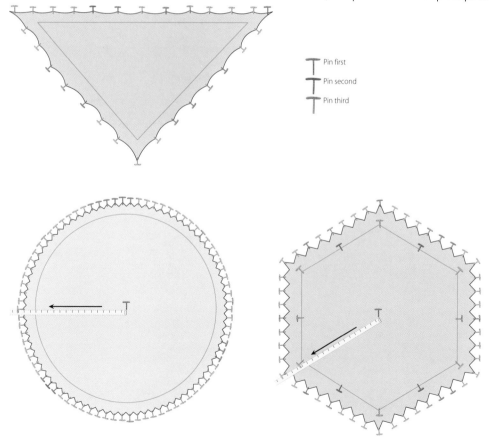

Yarns Used In Projects

[1]

ALPACA WITH A TWIST *Fino (alpaca, silk; 100g; 875 yds)*

JADE SAPPHIRE *Lacey Lamb (extra fine lamb's wool; 60g; 825 yds)*

JADE SAPPHIRE *Mongolian Cashmere 2-ply (cashmere; 55g; 400 yds)*

JAGGERSPUN *Zephyr (wool, silk; 454g; 5040 yds)*

KARABELLA *Lightweight Cashmere (cashmere; 25g; 202 yds)*

LORNA'S LACES *Helen's Lace (silk, wool; 114g; 1250 yds)*

MISTI ALPACA *Lace 2-ply (baby alpaca; 50g; 437 yds)*

PATONS *Baby Merino (discontinued)*

HAND-DYED *20/2 silk*

HANDSPUN *2-ply Merino*

HANDSPUN *Hebridean*

[2]

HABU TEXTILES *2/10 Kusaki-Zome (silk; 28g; 155 yds)*

HABU TEXTILES *2/17 Tsumugi (silk; 50g; 265 yds)*

KNIT ONE, CROCHET TOO *Douceur et Soie (baby mohair, silk; 25g; 225 yds)*

NEEDFUL YARNS/LANA GATTO *Mohair Royal (kid mohair, nylon; 25g; 235 yds)*

TWISTED SISTERS *Petite Voodoo (silk, wool; 50g; 190 yds)*

WESTMINSTER/JAEGER *Alpaca 4-ply (alpaca; 50g; 202 yds)*

WESTMINSTER/ROWAN *Kidsilk Haze (super kid mohair, silk; 25g; 229 yds)*

2-PLY HAND-DYED *Silk*

20/2 HAND-DYED *Silk*

HANDSPUN *Merino/Cashmere*

HANDSPUN *Merino/Silk*

HANDSPUN *Polworth/Kid*

HANDSPUN *Silk*

[3]

COLINETTE *Tao (silk; 50g; 129 yds)*

FIESTA *La Luz (silk; 57g; 220 yds)*

SKACEL *Seta Bella (silk; 50g; 138 yds)*

8/2 HAND-DYED *Silk*

Other Yarn Choices

1

AURORA/ORNAGHI FILATI *Merino Oro (merino; 100g; 1250 yds)*

BELISA *Cashmere (cashmere; 50g; 500 yds)*

CASCADE/MADIL *Kid Seta (mohair, silk; 25g; 230 yds)*

CRYSTAL PALACE *Kid Merino (kid merino, nylon; 25g; 240 yds)*

HABU *1/13 Daijoshi (silk; 85g; 404 yds)*

JADE SAPPHIRE *Cashmere/Silk (cashmere, silk; 55g; 400 yds)*

JOJOLAND *2-Ply Cashmere (cashmere; 57g; 400 yds)*

KARABELLA *Lace Mohair (super kid mohair, polamid, wool; 50g; 540 yds)*

SKACEL *Merino Lace (merino; 100g; 1350 yds)*

TRENDSETTER *Cashwool (merino extrafine; 100g; 1460 yds)*

TWISTED SISTERS *Za Zu (extra fine merino; 50g; 390 yds)*

2

ALCHEMY *Haiku (mohair, silk; 25g; 325 yds)*

ALCHEMY *Silk Purse (silk; 50g; 138 yds)*

HABU *1/5 Silk Roving (wool, silk; 28g; 155 yds)*

JCA/ADRIENNE VITTADINI *Celia (silk; 25g; 109 yds)*

JOJOLAND *Melody (wool; 50g; 220yds)*

TAHKI • STACY CHARLES/FILATURA DI CROSA *Luxury (silk; 50g; 160 yds)*

TRENDSETTER *Super Kid Seta (superkid mohair, silk; 25g; 230 yds)*

TWISTED SISTERS *Lust (superkid mohair, silk; 50g; 460 yds)*

TWISTED SISTERS *Mojo (kid mohair; 50g; 200 yds)*

3

ALCHEMY *Bamboo (bamboo; 50g; 150 yds)*

BLUE SKY ALPACAS *Alpaca & Silk (alpaca, silk; 50g; 146 yds)*

CLASSIC ELITE *Interlude (linen, silk; 50g; 82 yds)*

DEBBIE BLISS *Cotton Cashmere (cotton, cashmere; 50g; 103 yds)*

GREAT ADIRONDACK *Silk Noir (silk; 229g; 900 yds)*

HABU *1/6 Bamboo (bamboo; 85g; 186 yds)*

SOUTH WEST TRADING COMPANY *Pure (soysilk; 50g; 149 yds)*

TILLI TOMAS *Pure and Simple (soysilk; 100g; 260 yds)*

Many wonderful yarns are available for knitting today's lace. The colors are sophisticated and vivid, and their range is often extensive. The fibers are among the most luxurious to wear and pleasurable to knit. We were not able to incorporate them all in our projects, so include a listing of other yarns we have enjoyed sampling. You need not fear substituting yarns. Choose a yarn and color you love. Buy a ball, work a swatch or two, block, and make your decision.

What makes a needle especially suited for lace knitting? Choose a non-slippery material (often wood or bamboo), well-tapered points, and smooth joins between the needles and cable of a circular needle. Usually you will use a needle a size or two larger than you would normally use for a yarn.

For updates, see knittinguniverse.com/VLT/

NEEDLES

US	MM	UK
0	2	14
1	2.25	–
2	2.75	12
3	3.25	10
4	3.5	–
5	3.75	9
6	4	8
7	4.5	7
8	5	6
9	5.5	5
10	6	4
10½	6.5	3
11	8	0
13	9	00
15	10	000

Old UK sizes
with metric equivalent *

Size 16	1.829mm
Size 18	1.219mm
Size 20	0.914mm
Size 22	0.711mm
Size 24	0.559mm
Size 26	0.457mm

* Miss Lambert's Standard Filière with sizes 1–28 was patented in 1847, and the standardizing of needle sizes was underway. Treat all early size notations as suspect.

Understanding Lace & Charts

In most lace patterns, the number of stitches remains constant on each row. In these cases, when a yarn-over adds a stitch, a decrease removes another stitch. This yarn-over and decrease combination is called a pair.

A single yarn-over can be paired with a single decrease; 2 single yarn-overs can be paired with a double decrease.

The decreases used in lace patterns are few and familiar. The variety of patterns comes from the placement of yarn-overs and decreases. Most often both parts of the pair are on the same row and side by side, but they also can be separated by other stitches (Chart E). In some patterns, yarn-overs are on one row, decreases on another (Chart A).

Reading charts

Charts are invaluable when following the yarn-over/decrease relationships that are so crucial to the success and pleasure of lace knitting. If you're a beginning lace knitter or have had problems with lace, give charted patterns a try.

Each square of the chart is one stitch (or one knitting operation, such as a k2tog or an SK2P). Each row of the chart shows a completed row of knitting.

The chart represents the right side of the fabric, so check the key to see how to work a certain symbol on the right side and on the wrong side.

Read the chart in the same direction as you knit: the rows from bottom to top, right-side rows from right to left, wrong-side rows from left to right. (In circular knitting, all rows are right-side rows, therefore the chart is always read from right to left.)

Heavy lines set off a pattern repeat from any partial repeats or edge stitches. They function in the same way that asterisks do. In Chart E work the first 12 stitches of the chart, work the 10-stitch repeat until only 3 stitches remain, then work the last 3 stitches of the chart.

The slant of a decrease is clear from a chart. The symbol for a k2tog slants to the right; the symbol for an SSK slants to the left. Early knitting instructions only use the k2tog decrease (Charts A and E). As the century progressed, left-slanting decreases were added; Chart B shows this use of directional decreases. Compare the decreases highlighted with yellow on charts B and E.

Each right-side row has yarn-over/decrease pairs plus an extra yarn-over, resulting in an increase on the left edge. These 3 extra stitches are bound off on Row 12.

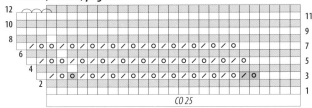

Chart A, Border, page 80

Chart A Cast on 25 sts
Row 1 (RS) Knit.
Row 2 Knit.
Row 3 K4, (yo, k2tog) 9 times, yo twice, k2tog, k1.
Row 4,6,8 K3, p1, knit to end.
Row 5 K5, (yo, k2tog) 9 times, yo twice, k2tog, k1.
Row 7 K6, (yo, k2tog) 9 times, yo twice, k2tog, k1.
Rows 9–11 Knit.
Row 12 Bind off 3 sts, knit to end.

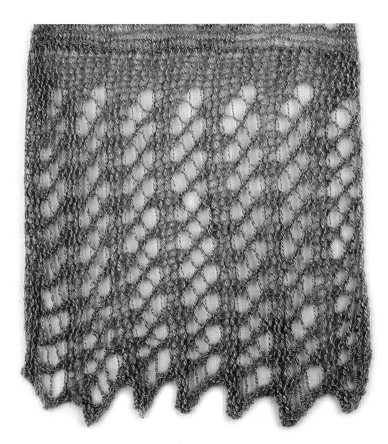

It's simple to see the pairs here; an example of each is highlighted in orange. The SK2P is a double decrease and pairs with 2 yarn-overs. The decreases highlighted in yellow are **directional**.

Stitch Key

- ☐ K on RS, p on WS
- ☐ P on RS, k on WS
- ◿ K2tog on RS; p2tog on WS
- ◿ K3tog
- ◿ P2tog on RS, k2 tog on WS
- △ P3tog
- ◺ SSK on RS
  SSP on WS
- △ S2KP2
- ◣ SK2P
- ▲ SK3P
- ◉ Yo
- ⅄ K in F&B of st on RS,
  p in F&B of st on WS
- ⅄ M1
- ⌒ Bind off 1 st
- ▨ Sts do not exist in this area of chart
- ▽ Slip st purlwise with yarn at WS
- ⌄ Slip st purlwise with yarn at RS
- Ω K st tbl

  If a symbol is red, pay attention to the unusual action defined for that stitch. If a row number is red, pay attention for a different instruction when working that row. Occasionally a pattern requires a special symbol; it will be defined in the key.

Here the yarn-overs and decreases are on the same line but often separated by 1 or 2 stitches. The decreases highlighted in yellow are **non-directional**.

Chart B, Small diamond, Gaugain, page 60

9-st repeat
10-row repeat

Chart B Multiple of 9 sts + 8
Row 1 (RS) K4, *k2, k2tog, yo, k1, yo, SSK, k2; repeat from*, k4.
Row 2 and all WS rows Purl.
Row 3 K4, *k1, k2tog, yo, k3, yo, SSK, k1; repeat from*, k4.
Row 5 K4, *k2tog, yo, k5, yo, SSK; repeat from*, k4.
Row 7 K4, *k2, yo, SSK, k1, k2tog, yo, k2; repeat from*, k4.
Row 9 K4, *k3, yo, SK2P, yo, k3; repeat from*, k4.
Repeat Rows 1–12.

Chart E, Small leaf, Lambert, page 61

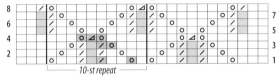

10-st repeat

Chart E Multiple of 10 sts + 15
Row 1 (RS) K2, *k1, yo, k2, k2tog, p1, k2tog, k2, yo; repeat from*, k3.
Row 2 (WS) P3, *p1, yo, p1, p2tog, k1, p2tog, p1, yo, p2; repeat from*, p2.
Row 3 K2, *k3, yo, k2tog, p1, k2tog, yo, k2; repeat from*, k3.
Row 4 P3, *p3, yo, p3tog, yo, p4; repeat from*, p2.
Row 5 K2, *p1, k2tog, k2, yo, k1, yo, k2, k2tog; repeat from*, p1, k2.
Row 6 P2, k1, *p2tog, p1, yo, p3, yo, p1, p2tog, k1; repeat from*, p2.
Row 7 K2, *p1 k2tog, yo, k5, yo, k2tog; repeat from*, p1, k2.
Row 8 P2, p2tog, *yo, p7, yo, p3tog; repeat from*, yo, p7, yo, p2tog, p2.

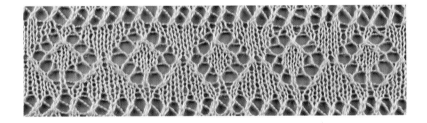

TIPS

• Practice these patterns from charts working with a light weight yarn and needles that are 1 to 2 sizes larger than usual. Cast on the number of stitches necessary for one or two pattern repeats plus border stitches. Watch how the increases and decreases align. You will soon make a friend of the pattern and charts will be your knitting language of choice.

• To read charts more easily, use a magnetic board such as those sold for counted cross-stitch. Photo copy the pattern page(s) and increase the print size 200% so it is easier to read at a distance. Place the board under the pattern, and use the magnetic rule to mark each row as you knit. The ultimate is a book rest on your knee and magnetic board on the book rest. This will accelerate knitting speed and reduce irritability.

• Charts make it easy to understand a pattern stitch before you knit it; to recognize, avoid, and correct errors; to enlarge or reduce a pattern stitch; to combine pattern stitches or their elements. (See Lace Design and How to make your own wide border, pages 180-183.)

• Use markers between the repeats of a pattern. For fine yarns, simply fold about 8" of contrast yarn in half and knot the loop to fit needle.

• For a review of working yarn-overs, see page 169.

• If you run into a problem with the stitch count in a row, check for a missing yarn-over in the preceding row. To pick-up a missing yarn-over, see page 169.

• To begin your exploration of lace knitting, start with the charts marked with an * in the project index, page 196.

Designing your own shawl can be
as simple as choosing a different
yarn and adding a new border.

For a completely different look,
see page 30.

178

Design your own
Change the border

A ruffled handsome border

This shawl is worked in Rowan's Kidsilk Haze in color 579 Splendour following the instructions on page 32, EXCEPT after Row 212, do not bind off. **Next row** (RS) P5, increase 1, [* p5, k1; repeat from * 3 times, p4, yo, k1] repeat until 2 stitches from center, p2; increase 1; p2, [k1, yo, p4, * k1, p5; repeat from * 3 times] repeat until 5 stitches remain, increase 1, p5. This establishes the Bell ruffle. Work Rows 2–24 of Bell ruffle chart. Bind off.

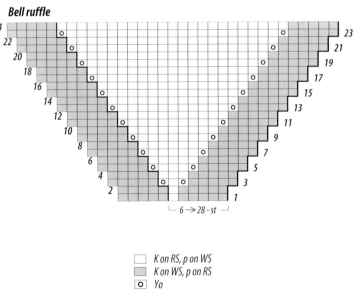

Bell ruffle

6 → 28 - st

☐ K on RS, p on WS
▨ K on WS, p on RS
◉ Yo

179

Lace Design

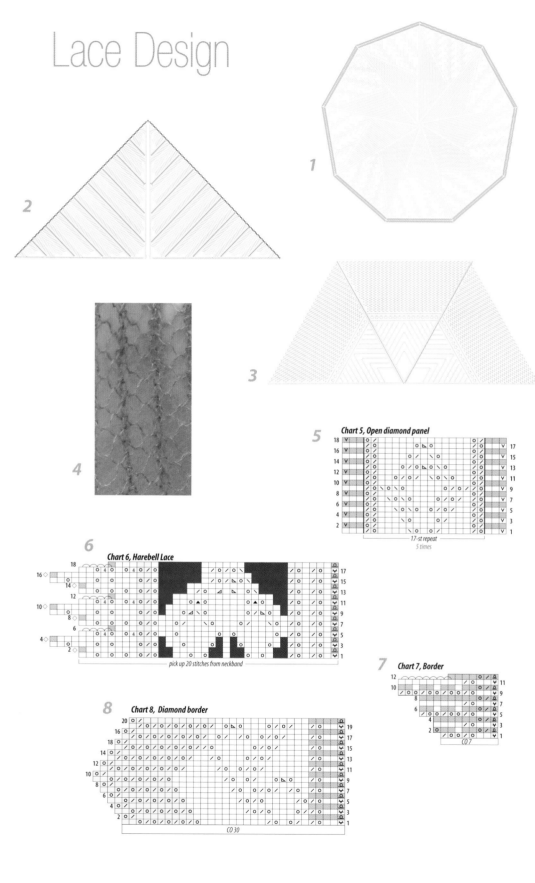

Chart 5, Open diamond panel

17-st repeat
5 times

Chart 6, Harebell Lace

pick up 20 stitches from neckband

Chart 7, Border

CO 7

Chart 8, Diamond border

CO 30

We began understanding lace design by understanding the simple increases and decreases producing the triangles of Vandyke borders (page 4).
Elongating the simple border produces a triangular fichu or shawl as in the stretched triangle fichu *(page 8)*.

1 Nine rather simple triangles (one half a Vandyke border) knit circularly produce the quite complex looking cap shawl *(page 28)*.

Mirroring yarn-over increases on two sides of a center line produces the standard triangular shawl: with increases on the edge of the Syrian shawl *(page 130)*, or increases inside border stitches on the cherry leaf shawl *(page 134)*.

2 The handsome triangle shawl *(page 32)* is two triangles worked side-by-side, from the center of the neck, out and down.

3 Spider-web shawls *(page 44)* are made with 3 standard triangles side-by-side for the half-hexagon and fichu or 6 triangles knit around for the full hexagon. All three are closely related to the simple triangle of the Syrian shawl - with only the direction of paired eyelets reversed.

FAGGOTING IN CENTER PATTERNS
When arranged vertically or diagonally, the yo-k2tog pair and its variations are known as faggoting.

4 The entire center of the first bordered scarf *(page 16)* is simple, centered faggoting (all rows worked in pattern).

The opera fichu *(page 122)* shows faggoting in lace knitting (alternate rows worked in pattern).

Both the diamond *(page 104)* and Dolphin lace *(page 106)* double-bordered scarves have centered faggoting between alternating borders.

5 Straight lines of faggoting often separate other lace motifs. The handsome triangle shawl *(page 32)* shows lines of faggoting between each motif, as does the melon shawl *(page 146)*, stripes and torchon lace *(page 158)*, and the Maltese shawl *(page 162)*.

Zigzag lines of faggoting can outline another motif as in the leaf and trellis design *(page 54)*.

6 The entire center panel can be outlined or framed with faggoting, as in the pink sampler *(page 58)*, the Pyrenees shawl *(page 68)*, and the Harebell fichu *(page 118)*.

FAGGOTING ON BORDERS
Faggoting on the outside of borders

7 Faggoting can be the entire border, as in Mrs. Hope's Vandyke border *(page 4)*, Miss Lambert's Vandyke border *(page 50)* and the Maltese shawl *(page 162)*.

8 Or faggoting can border another lace motif, as in the leaf and trellis shawl *(page 54)*, the scarf with No. 20 edging *(page 84)*, and scarf with edging 21 *(page 100)*.

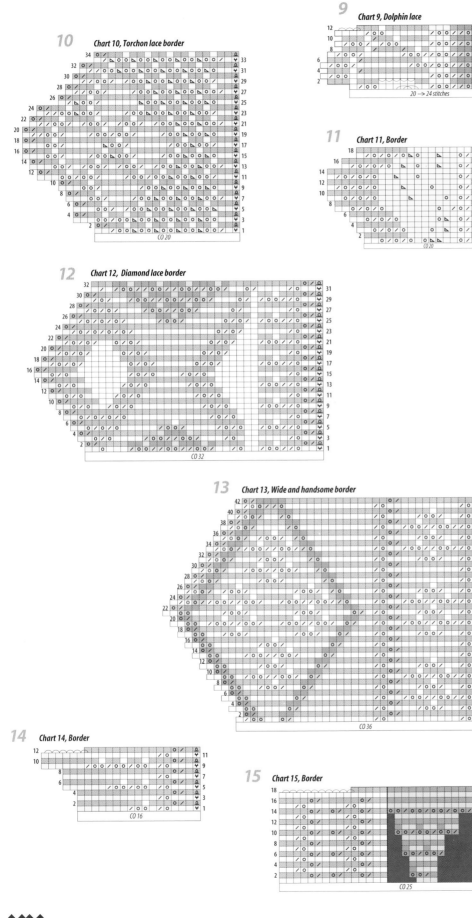

10 *Chart 10, Torchon lace border*

CO 20

9 *Chart 9, Dolphin lace*

20 → 24 stitches

11 *Chart 11, Border*

CO 20

12 *Chart 12, Diamond lace border*

CO 32

13 *Chart 13, Wide and handsome border*

CO 36

14 *Chart 14, Border*

CO 16

15 *Chart 15, Border*

CO 25

Faggoting and eyelets inside border patterns accentuate an outer border pattern.

Single faggoting is seen in the wide border for the spider pattern *(page 24)*, scarf with No. 20 edging *(page 84)*, and many single lines of faggoting in the Victorian ruby scarf *(page 92)*.

9 One or more lines of double faggoting is even more common: Miss Lambert's Vandyke border *(page 50)*, leaf and trellis border *(page 54)*, wide and handsome border *(page 88)*, open and solid diamond *(page 90)*, Dolphin lace *(page 106)*, and melon border *(page 146)*.

10 Eyelets or faggoting can surround a border pattern, as in the Clarence border *(page 82)* or stripes and torchon lace *(page 158)*.

COMBINATIONS

Faggoting, center pattern motifs, or stripes can extend and define lace sections in center patterns or extend the border. It is easiest (but not necessary) to begin with motifs with the same number of rows in their repeats. Two-row faggoting is the easiest to align with any other pattern and the most widely used design element.

Faggoting within the center pattern can be repeated in the border: seen in the spider pattern *(page 24)* and the Melon border *(page 146)*.

11 Center pattern motifs can be repeated in the border: also in the wide border in spider pattern *(page 24)*, the leaf and trellis *(page 54)*, as well as diamonds and triangles *(page 150)*.

12 Lines of faggoting may be combined with background faggoting as in the open and solid diamond *(page 90)* and scarf with edging 21 *(page 100)*.

13 Nearly any center pattern motif can be isolated, defined with faggoting stripes or zigzag edges, and turned into a border: wide border in spider net lace *(page 24)*, wide and handsome border *(page 88)*, and Victorian ruby *(page 92)*.

14 The traditional Vandyke border *(chart 7 and page 50)* can be placed inside a solid edging as in the cape *(page 114)* and the melon shawl *(page 146)*.

15 Ornate, shaped border patterns can be placed between double or triple faggoting as in the Harebell lace sandwiched between faggoting *(chart 6 and page 119)* or the spectacular derivation of Vandyke lace between double and triple faggoting in the Victoria shawl *(page 154)*. Both of these borders are inspired!

Narrow border

Wide border, page 24

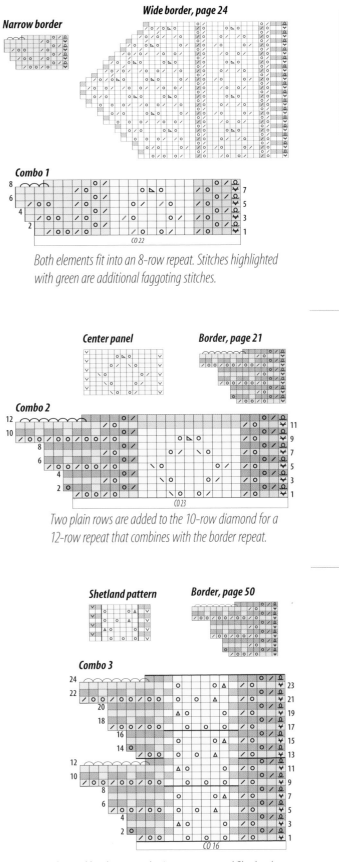

Combo 1

Both elements fit into an 8-row repeat. Stitches highlighted with green are additional faggoting stitches.

Center panel

Border, page 21

Combo 2

Two plain rows are added to the 10-row diamond for a 12-row repeat that combines with the border repeat.

Shetland pattern

Border, page 50

Combo 3

Original border pattern's 12-row repeat and Shetland pattern's 8-row repeat both fit into a 24-row repeat.

How to make your own wide border

You can combine lace elements to create your own wide borders. Charted patterns make the process easy. Just photocopy the charts you want to use; a scissors and removable clear tape make it easy to experiment.

All elements that you put together into one border will have to have the same number of rows for the border repeat to work. It is easiest to start with patterns that already have the same number of rows or that share a common multiple. If this is not the case, one of the patterns may need to be extended or reduced to make the number of rows fit with the other pattern(s).

Here are a few combinations that show how the process works.

Mrs. Hope's edging

Cornelia Mee's Veil, page 69

Combo 4

Mrs. Hope's 30-row edging is reduced to 22 rows to fit other elements.

Diamond lace border, page 90

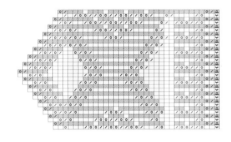

A section of a border can be repeated.

Other Borders

To encourage your further explorations, here are several more lace borders. Each chart is labeled with the page of one project for which it is a good alternative.

Note The instructions for knitting on the original border may need to be adapted for the new border's row-repeat and width. Refer to pages 184 and 185 for help with this.

1886 border, page 126

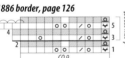

CO 9

Coburg border, page 162

CO 32

Narrow point border, page 25

CO 8

Wide point lace, page 130

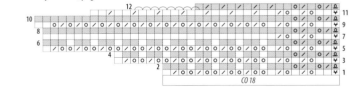

CO 18

Seashell border, page 146

CO 23

☐ K on RS, p on WS
▨ P on RS, k on WS
⟍ SSK
╱ K2tog (if worked on RS), p2tog (on WS)
╱ K2tog, or SSK for directional decrease
◿ K3tog (if worked on RS), p3tog (on WS)
◣ SK2P
△ S2KP2
◯ Yo
⊻ Sl1 with yarn at RS
⊽ Sl1 with yarn at WS
Ω K1 tbl
⌒ Bind off 1 st

 Melon st, see illustration on page 147

 K7, pass sts 1–6 over st 7
pass 4th, 5th and 6th sts
over first 3 sts

Planning a shawl with a knitted-on border

The Victorians knit borders separately, gathered the border to provide the extra length needed to round the corners, and sewed them onto the center panel of a shawl or scarf. We recommend joining a border to the center panel as you work the border. This process, referred to as knitting-on, is described on pages 174 and 175. It uses Single Joins along the sides and ends, Double and Triple Joins at the corners.

Planning your own shawl may simply involve choosing a yarn, a color, and a pattern. Or you may want to use a yarn of a different weight—a change in the scale of the pattern which may require a different number of center-panel repeats or a wider or narrower border. Or you may want to combine the border of one shawl with another's center panel (an approach used several times when developing the shawls for this book); or you may want to modify existing lace patterns; or you may want to adjust the shape. If so, you need to do a bit of planning.

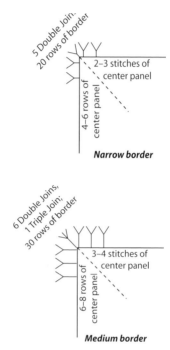

Narrow border

First, choose one center pattern or combine two or three in columns or bands. Cast on at least two or three repeats of your center pattern (plus 2 edge stitches plus any framing stitches) to check how you like the design in your gauge. Change needle sizes until you love your pattern, yarn, and gauge combination. Then cast on and work 2 or 3 repeats of your border pattern. (Remember to designate 1 or 2 selvedge stitches on both center pattern and border to permit clean slipped stitch edges.)

Work several repeats of the border you designed around your center-pattern swatch. Experiment with a combination of Single, Double and Triple Joins (page 174-5) to fit around the corner without distorting your border or center pattern. Rip the border and begin again if you are not perfectly pleased.

Medium border

Guidelines for fitting borders around corners
Borders are grouped into four main categories according to the number of stitches cast on:

Border type	Stitches cast on	Joins for corner	Border rows for corner
Narrow	9 or fewer	4 to 6 Double Joins	16 to 24 rows
Medium	10 to 20	6 to 8 Double and 1 Triple Join	30 to 38 rows
Wide	21 to 30	8 Double and 1 to 4 Triple Joins	38 to 56 rows
Extra Wide	30 or more	8 Double and 4 to 8 Triple Joins	56 to 80 rows

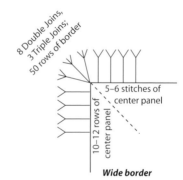

Since each Double Join involves 4 border rows and each Triple Join involves 6 border rows, wide and extra wide borders with very few rows in a repeat (striped border, page 80, or French trellis border, page 98), require many repeats to round the corner. A wide and tall border requires fewer repeats to round the corner (wide border in spider pattern, page 24).

Wide border

This spider net shawl makes a good example for fitting a wide and tall border to a small center pattern. Along the sides, one 32-row border repeat attaches 16 times to four 8-row shawl repeats. At the corners, 3 border repeats (48 attaching rows) connect to a total of only 25 side and top stitches, making an average of 16 attaching rows to 8 center stitches—twice as many border rows around the corner as on the straight sides of the shawl.

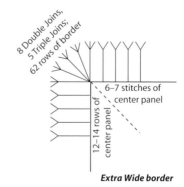

Block your sample as you wish to block your finished shawl. Measure width of border at widest point_____". Measure width _____" and height_____" of one center-pattern repeat.

Extra Wide border

Experience has now taught you enough to knit a perfectly beautiful shawl you will treasure. It is possible to cast on and work your design with no more information. However, if you wish a shawl of a specific size and with no surprises, work through the steps on the next page.

184

Bold type indicates numbers you provide from blocked swatches and desired dimensions.

Fill in those blanks, then work the formulas. Color coding makes it easy.

Blocked border width _____" x 2 = _____" border allowance

Desired shawl width _____" – border allowance _____" = _____" center-panel width

Center panel width _____" ÷ **blocked width of center-panel repeat** _____" = _____ # of repeats (round to nearest #)

# of repeats _____ x **stitches per repeat** _____ = _____ center-pattern stitches

Center-pattern stitches _____ + 2 edge stitches + any framing stitches * _____ = _____ stitches to cast on for center panel **

Desired shawl length _____" – border allowance _____" = _____" center panel length

Center-panel length _____" ÷ **blocked length of center-panel repeat** _____" = _____ # of repeats (round to nearest #)

# of repeats _____ x **rows per repeat** _____ = _____ pattern rows + any framing rows * _____ = _____ total center-panel

rows ÷ 2 = _____ slip stitches (or joins) on edge of center panel

Border rows per repeat _____ ÷ 2 = _____ slip stitches per border repeat

Knitting border onto sides of center panel

Slip stitches on edge of center panel _____ ÷ slip stitches per border repeat _____ =

_____ # of border repeats with remainder of ...._____ center-panel slip stitches

– 2 = _____ border repeats between corners **   ÷ 2 = _____ center-panel slip stitches to be added to a center-panel repeat at each corner

Knitting border onto top and bottom of center panel

Stitches in center panel _____ ÷ slip stitches per border repeat _____ =

_____ # of border repeats with remainder of ...._____ center-panel stitches

– 2 = _____ border repeats between corners **   ÷ 2 = _____ center-panel stitches to be added to a center-panel repeat at each corner

* Any garter, stockinette, or other stitch used to frame the center lace pattern.

** Remember, there is one fewer loop under the needle than cast-on stitches over the needle, so adjust
stitches in lace cast-on or in last row to make these numbers equal.

*** In most cases, at least two border repeats will be used plus any remaining slip stitches to attach border at corners; adjust if necessary.

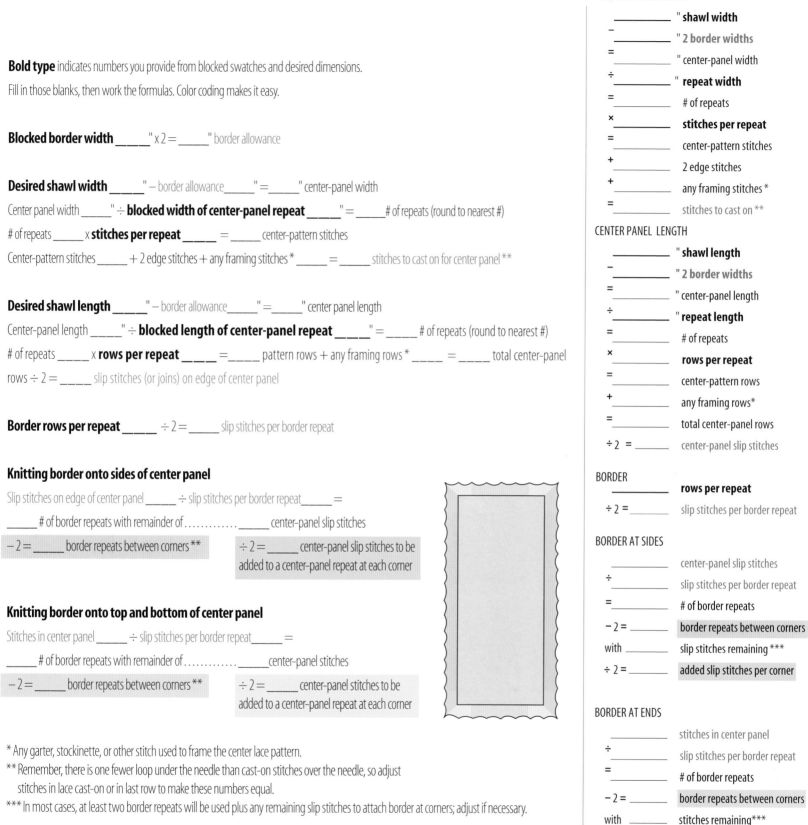

CENTER PANEL WIDTH

_____ " **shawl width**

– _____ " **2 border widths**

= _____ " center-panel width

÷ _____ " **repeat width**

= _____ # of repeats

× _____ **stitches per repeat**

= _____ center-pattern stitches

+ _____ 2 edge stitches

+ _____ any framing stitches *

= _____ stitches to cast on **

CENTER PANEL LENGTH

_____ " **shawl length**

– _____ " **2 border widths**

= _____ " center-panel length

÷ _____ " **repeat length**

= _____ # of repeats

× _____ **rows per repeat**

= _____ center-pattern rows

+ _____ any framing rows*

= _____ total center-panel rows

÷ 2 = _____ center-panel slip stitches

BORDER

_____ **rows per repeat**

÷ 2 = _____ slip stitches per border repeat

BORDER AT SIDES

_____ center-panel slip stitches

÷ _____ slip stitches per border repeat

= _____ # of border repeats

– 2 = _____ border repeats between corners

with _____ slip stitches remaining ***

÷ 2 = _____ added slip stitches per corner

BORDER AT ENDS

_____ stitches in center panel

÷ _____ slip stitches per border repeat

= _____ # of border repeats

– 2 = _____ border repeats between corners

with _____ stitches remaining***

÷ 2 = _____ added stitches per corner

Belton House

Bridge of Sighs

ON LOCATION   ON LOCATION   ON LOCATION

Belton House Orangery   King's Chapel

Street scene–Cambridge   Cambridge houses   Roses in an English garden   Tudor Courtyard   West entrance–Belton House   Belton House gate

Belton House lawn and garden

Lavenham

The River Cam

A quiet passage

Cloisters at Queen's College

Cambridge—The Senate House

King's College Chapel   Back of Queen's College

COLOPHON:
Jane Sowerby's Victorian Adventure

In Stonely, just west of Cambridge, in East Anglia, Jane Sowerby's home is chock-full of shawls. They're stuffed in a large wooden trunk, draped on beds and chairs, festooned from lamps, hanging from curtain rods, cascading from hangers, covering the floor.

Shawls haven't just taken over Jane's home, but her life. "These shawls are my babies," Jane says. "Hundreds and hundreds of hours have gone into all the charting and knitting. I know it may sound peculiar, but I feel almost that I've gone back into that era, to the people who knitted them. I've sieved through their patterns, taken them apart, corrected their mistakes. By the time I finished many of these shawls, it was almost like I had given birth to them.

"It was an evolving process, never really intended to be a book; that just happened. I did one shawl, then another, and it was like, 'I *must* do another, I can't see the end of this yet.' It became an obsession. There seemed to be an avalanche of Victorian knitting patterns waiting to be found. Everybody was knitting then—including the Queen—it was the *in* thing.

"So I got myself a reader's card at the British Library in London, the equivalent of The Library of Congress in Washington, and started doing research. I found *Weldon's Practical Knitter*, and other early knitting writers. One of them produced ten books in ten years! These weren't the Victorian wallflowers we assume women were at that time. These were career women—not Victorian-wife stereotypes, warming their husband's slippers—who didn't care about Victorian

(Opposite page, clockwise from bottom left) The longest-reigning British monarch held the royal scepter and orb—and knitting needles—The Queen Victoria Memorial. Symbols of an age—gilded gates of Kensington Palace, Queen Victoria's birthplace; a pub sign portraying her majesty; "V & A's" everywhere: intertwined monograms carved on the gates of Buckingham Palace, the most famous V & A, the Victoria & Albert Museum, embellishing a lamp on the Victorian Embankment; the gleaming Prince Albert Memorial; iron Victorian floral motif; an icon of the Underground, Victoria Station; Lavenham's 16th century Guildhall, half-timbered framing on a grand scale.

 (This page, from top), Author Jane Sowerby, in the garden at Belton House; Belton House, the magnificent 17th century, 1,300 acre, Lincolnshire manor familiar to Jane Austen fans as Lady Catherine de Bourgh's Rosings Park in the BBC's 1995 'Pride and Prejudice.'

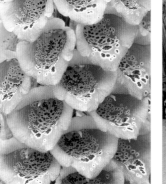

convention, and did what they wanted. I really admired them—and I really wanted to learn more.

"When you read their books, you begin to absorb a little of the character of the person. Most of these women seem determined, dogmatic characters, and you can almost imagine them rapping your knuckles if you made a mistake. They're very prim and proper, even though their patterns may not always be clear or correct, so difficult to understand. Nobody had ever done this before: there was no system for abbreviations, pattern instructions, for drawing charts. They had nothing. They had to start at the beginning. I felt a kind of duty to have their voices heard.

"It was a learning process, and their books gradually got better. Still, for a modern knitter, deciphering it all would be just dreadful: now we say, 'Knit 2tog 17 times.' This was 1840, and they would write, 'Knit 2 together' *literally* seventeen times, and it might take many lines. I used to get dizzy reading some of these patterns, it was a nightmare. Even up to 1886, it was all there, but you had to be *so* on the ball. I can imagine those knitters in groups, in their drawing rooms, in the afternoon, trying to decipher these patterns. I can't imagine lone knitters would have got anything else done, because it took *me* hours and hours and hours. Once I broke them down, I realized the patterns were incredibly simple.

"The Victorians went in for hugely strong colors, much stronger than those of my shawls, actually. There was a change going on from natural to chemical dyes, so the colors became a lot bolder. I chose bright colors that the Victorians would have loved, but I also love natural colors and fibers, and yarns that make a fashion statement. That's why I wanted to see these Victorian shawls brought to life, into the 21st century—not have them look like lovely museum pieces. Your idea of photographing them on models, in historic settings, is perfect. At the time these patterns were written, a black and white engraving is all a knitter got to see. From that point of view, if one of these knitting writers came back to our photo shoot as a ghost, I should imagine she would be thrilled to bits."

Could any visiting apparition be half as thrilled as Jane's visiting photographer at seeing the glossy postcards, brochures, fliers, and leaflets filled with story-book locations? This feast—along with a cup of tea—awaits at Jane's table: 'Melford Hall, one of the most satisfying Elizabethan Houses in East Anglia, built sometime between 1554 and 1578...' 'Kentwell Hall & Gardens, a little great house of magical beauty, one of the loveliest Elizabethan Houses...' 'Audley End House & Gardens, one of the most magnificent stately homes in England...' 'Peckover House & Garden, a lovely Georgian brick town house, with a charming two acre Victorian walled garden: herbaceous borders, roses, orangery, fernery, and delightful summerhouses...' 'Newby Hall & Gardens, one of Yorkshire's renowned houses, a very fine example of 18th century

(Clockwise, from above) Dressed in purple: at Hyde Park, and the Royal Albert Hall; lions guard a fountain at Belton House; the 1830 orangery, and a quiet spot in its greenery; a lacy passion flower; a Grecian temple at Kew Gardens; orangery pool residents; a fern unfurls; crowned in ferns; Belton House Regency interiors; a photo shoot among the topiary; self-powered lawn mower.

interior decoration: Gobelin's Tapestry Room, a gallery of classical statuary, some of Chippendale's finest furniture, 25 acres of award-winning gardens full of rare and beautiful plants . . .' 'Oxburgh Hall, Norfolk, a magnificent moated house, with a great Tudor gatehouse, built in 1482 . . .'.

The next magnificent location—"Belton House, Grantham, Lincolnshire, undoubtedly one of the finest examples of Restoration domestic architecture with 36 acres of gardens . . ."—looks familiar, and the brochure tells you why: "Opening of the refurbished Blue Bedroom and Dressing Room: you may recall Mr. Darcy writing to Miss Bennett at the desk in this bedroom in the BBC's *Pride and Prejudice* . . ."

Jane Austen? You can imagine the excitement of this English-major-turned-photographer. With Jane's husband, David, at the wheel, you're out the door, heading north on the A1, on the 'wrong' side of the road. Does one ever get used to driving on the left, you wonder. But not for long. The murmur of the engine, the relaxing drive through fields covered with yellow oil seed rape in full bloom, and the jet lag, put you to sleep.

When Jane awakens you, you're driving through the winding streets of Grantham, about an hour north of Stonely. Soon you spot a familiar sign that bears the oak leaves logo of the National Trust, the conservation charity which 'protects special places in England, Wales, and Northern Ireland, for ever, for everyone.' The 1,300 wooded acres of *this* special place, Belton House, are dotted with wildflowers: bluebells, primroses, daffodils, cowslips, snowdrops, and forget-me-nots. After the gatehouse, you reach what appears to be the mansion. But, as it turns out, this grand building featuring niches, tall windows, and pedimented doorways is the former stables that now houses a restaurant. It's cloudy and rather chilly, and Jane suggests lunch and a cup of tea.

"It has been quite wet here lately," she says, and your heart skips a beat at the thought of rain during your upcoming photo shoot. But thoughts of inclement weather vanish as you walk across the immense lawn that spreads in front of Belton House. When, after about ten minutes, you stop and look back, the incredible view takes your breath away. Belton House stands amidst a sea of green, its magnificent golden façade punctuated with acres of glass. A central pediment crowns the front of the house, an airy cupola soars above six gables and eight tall chimneys, and a carved balustrade runs the length of the roof, lending a lacy feel to this impressive, stately home.

Jane has brought along a few shawls, and she's encouraged to stand in for a model. She walks up the front steps and smiles on cue, but the clouds that fill the sky darken the light, and it casts harsh, unpleasant shadows across her face. When we do this for real, you think, you'll *have* to have sun. And what about all those tourists in those bright raincoats? Perhaps, a telephoto lens with a very narrow angle of view would leave most of them out of your picture?

(Counterclockwise, from right) Belton House portrait; orangery oranges; Belton House façade, transformed into a lace niche; Kew Gardens temple; a yellow beauty; lacy leaves; author at rest; among the dahlias; Queen Anne's lace; a cactus bloom.

191

But there's no time to contemplate these photographic niceties. It's time to resume what Jane calls our 'reccy' (short for 'reconnoiter'). Through picturesque country lanes bordered with—honestly—Queen Anne's lace, we drive on. If there were any remotely suitable location within a day's drive of Stonely, you saw it: windmills in Suffolk, lighthouses in East Anglia, a lace museum and lace villages in Bedfordshire, timber-frame houses in historic Lavenham. And then there was Cambridge.

Cambridge dates from Roman times, growing where the road crossed the River Cam (hence its name). It has been home to dons and students for over 700 years: the mathematician Isaac Newton; the naturalist Charles Darwin; the diarist Samuel Pepys; the poet John Milton; and John Harvard, a student who went on to found his own college in the New World, just as so many English Kings and Queens had done at his alma mater. Cambridge is filled with magnificent Tudor, Medieval, and Gothic buildings, and their sculpted pinnacles resemble golden lace borders against the blue sky. Even the incomparable fan-vaulted ceiling of the King's College Chapel—completed by King Henry the VIII in 1515 and home to the world-famous King's College Singers—seems to be made up of lace carved in stone.

"It is impossible not to marvel at the skills of builders all those years ago," Jane says. "You're walking down the narrow lane that leads from King's College Chapel to King's Parade, the busy heart of the city. I love it here: the atmosphere of activity, the bicycles, the eccentricity, the visitors, the students. Cambridge is a city which is truly alive."

But Cambridge's town and gown bustle is only a memory as you cross the river and reach The Backs, the college lawns and green fields that border the Cam. Here, amidst the willows and gardens that line the riverbanks, King's Parade is replaced by another: that of waterfowl and punts gliding below. These flat-bottomed boats are propelled, gondola-like, usually by a college student who finds gainful employment as punt chauffeur. It's an idyllic scene of lazy school days, but a bucolic one as well—cattle graze near King's College Chapel.

"The sight of the morning or evening mist rising along The Backs and their beautiful gardens, is so memorable," Jane says. "The River Cam runs behind Queen's, King's, Trinity, and St. John's Colleges, and I've contacted them about shooting there. They have been quite nice, but being very academic, they wondered what the connection is with lace. So I explained what you said about the colleges' architecture complementing Victorian lace."

You're tracing your steps through Cambridge again, but a few months have elapsed, and now you and Jane are joined by the XRX photo team: Editor Elaine Rowley, Photo Stylist Rick Mondragon, Second Photographer Mike Winkleman, and Photographer Alexis Xenakis. And every day, the train from King's Cross brings a new lovely model from London. "Is this photo shoot going to be anything like the absolutely frantic pace of our reccy?" Jane asks with a laugh.

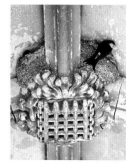

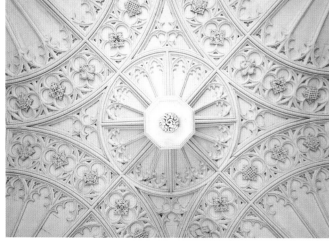

(Clockwise, from above) A lacy, fan-vaulted ceiling; one of the finest examples of English Medieval architecture, King's College Chapel, completed by King Henry the VIII; bridges to academe: the Bridge of Sighs, the Mathematical Bridge, Clare College Bridge; the Tudor Courtyard and Cloisters at Queen's; St. John's; King Henry VIII, his emblem, the portcullis, and swallows.

"I've never seen anything like it. I was lagging behind by day two. It was absolutely exhausting!"

But who can rush through the beauty of Queen's College—founded by Lady Margaret Beaufort, mother of Henry VII, and Elizabeth Woodville, wife of Edward IV? Time seems to stop in the stillness of the Cloister Court. A model, wrapped in a shawl, stands between ancient wood columns that support a half-timbered alcove; a shawl is draped on the centuries-old wooden steps that Erasmus once climbed on his way to his chambers; a bright scarf vies for attention with muted hydrangeas; an author writes in her journal.

Under the nearby Mathematical Bridge, a model steps onto a punt and poses, seemingly surrounded by water. But the punt is chained to the bank, and it's only through Rick and Mike's exertions that it seems to be floating down the Cam *(see photo, above)*.

In St. John's College—also founded by Lady Margaret—the picturesque Bridge of Sighs, an echo of its Venetian inspiration, is mirrored in the Cam; the Kitchen Bridge provides a backdrop for a shawl; and the quadrangle with its columned arches becomes an ideal setting for lace scarves.

And along the way, there were so many gilded statues to photograph, so many fantastical carvings, so many arched doorways, so many old clocks and sundials, so many flowers. But by now the sun—did anyone mention the sun? In all there were, count them, fourteen consecutive days of sunshine!—had fallen behind the tall trees that grow along The Backs, shading the cows grazing there, and bathing King's College Chapel in the softest gold *(see photo, opposite page)*. It is a short drive through Cambridge to our quarters near the rail station. Another model and another day at Belton House await.

As does our author, with her station wagon stuffed with lunch baskets, a portable stool, and her ever-present journal. You'd think Jane's hand is somehow guided by an unseen one—her journal entries would make any Victorian proud: "Monday, 6th September: Belton House is ours while closed to tourists. It is now owned by the National Trust, but once was the home of the Brownlows, from the 16th century. It is surrounded by beautiful parkland, with a wonderful long straight driveway for carriages which leads to the front entrance. Sheep graze peacefully in the fields round about, and the silence is magical. For two days we had the grounds to ourselves—courtesy of the wonderful staff and The National Trust—and were transported into another world. The team wandered at will, giving out exclamations of delight as they found new places to photograph.

"There had been thunderstorms the night before, and an early mist shrouded the landscape, soon to be replaced by more sunshine. The orangery, built in the 1830s,

(Counterclockwise, from above) Cows graze on The Backs—when not sheltering from the rain under a giant umbrella; punts anchored to terra firma; modeling on the water, and by the River Cam; a punt chauffeur; Trinity College's other attendees; prepping a shot; a lord and lady at Hampton Court; lace dandies; draped in lace; the country home of Thomas Lester, Lace Merchant.

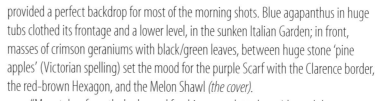

provided a perfect backdrop for most of the morning shots. Blue agapanthus in huge tubs clothed its frontage and a lower level, in the sunken Italian Garden; in front, masses of crimson geraniums with black/green leaves, between huge stone 'pine apples' (Victorian spelling) set the mood for the purple Scarf with the Clarence border, the red-brown Hexagon, and the Melon Shawl *(the cover)*.

"More tubs of myrtle, herbs, and fuschias were dotted outside, and the orangery itself was full of exotic Victorian plants, which in those days would have been brought back from The Grand Tour. There was even an indoor pond, in front of which Elaine sat eating her lunch and enjoying the cool shade of massive ferns. The rest of the team spread out on the orangery steps, and, for a short time, we all had escaped into another world."

Fortified by Jane's sandwiches, Mike gets adventuresome: "The afternoon comes, and there's a tense moment as Mike hovers precipitously over the pool of the lion's mouth fountain trying to hang the cream Sampler on the wall above. He makes it without falling in—and the shawl stays dry. Sighs of relief all around! In front of the fountain with its faded red-pink plasterwork, Patricia models the Beginner's Sampler with the sound of running water in the background.

"Next, more shots in front of the round pond surrounded by blue Veronica and yellow tagites, and, finally, under the archway below the clock tower Miss Lambert's Shetland Shawl, with a flowing charcoal silk skirt. The light is now growing softer, and another day of shooting is drawing to a close.

"Tuesday, 6th September: Another day at Belton. Still hot, but clouds over at the end of the afternoon. Alexis tries to get some indoor shots before we lose the light."

'Some indoor shots,' include an hour or so in the Blue Bedroom of Mr. Darcy (Colin Firth). Getting there means walking up dark staircases, down long corridors, through grand rooms. Your guide's flashlight reveals traces of fine plasterwork, exquisite wood carvings, rich tapestries, veined marble floors, brass balustrades, tall clocks, and Regency furniture, and, for a moment, Belton House resembles an elaborately appointed movie set.

When your guide throws open the tall shutters of the Blue Bedroom, shafts of sunlight pierce the darkness and this splendid room, with its bed's soaring canopy *(see photo, right)* becomes the setting for the Alpine Knit Scarf *(see page 34)*. Your last memory of Belton House outlined against a velvet sky, is from the edge of the oval driveway, where you take your last shot. Patricia, wearing the Shetland shawl, throws open her arms—and, with Belton House as your backdrop, you have your back cover. Then it is time to say goodbye to the magical world of Belton House and its friendly, welcoming staff, and say hello to Maria, who is arriving tonight in Cambridge.

(Clockwise, from above) The manicured gardens of Belton House; a marble nymph; a stone lion; a blooming lace bush; a model poses where once Elizabeth Bennett (Jennifer Ehle) strolled; on a pedestal: a red shawl, a photo stylist, a triangular scarf; grand staircases; a carriage arch; an author stands in for a model, works just one more row; the soaring Belton House—Blue Bedroom, but no Darcy (Colin Firth).

194

"Cambridge is shrouded by the early morning mist," Jane writes in her journal, "but by the time we arrive at Lavenham, in Suffolk, at 9:15 a.m., the sun has just broken through, giving a bright, but mellow, autumn light. Fourteenth and sixteenth century houses are everywhere, some painted in pale pastel shades, always in traditional Suffolk colors. Lavenham is a tiny old wool town steeped in history, originally the home of wool merchants, yeomen farmers, and cottage hand spinners. Maria models the red rose-leaf triangle on the steps of Mrs. Hardy's house, No. 8 High Street, whilst the church bells ring and most of the town is only just waking up.

"Later in the morning Maria wears the yellow Victoria shawl and red Scarf No. 8 in front of the Greyhound Pub, where red-hot geraniums drip from hanging baskets. It isn't just the flowers that are hot—we are too, as the day progresses and the sun shines relentlessly. It is a true English heat-wave, with temperatures around 90 degrees Fahrenheit. Although East Anglia is reputed to be the driest area in the United Kingdom, this summer has been unpredictable, and we kept our fingers crossed in case the weather changed, especially after the XRX team landed at Heathrow.

"By lunchtime, the town begins to get very busy (it's a popular tourist spot) and a playful wind gets up, which makes photography difficult. But, somehow, the sampler shawl moves with the breeze, with great shots in front of the Merchant's Row. A faded oak doorway provides another beautiful backdrop. After lunch at the Swan, under a shady tree in the garden, the team advances into Church Street, Water Street, and Lady Street where it is quieter. By 3:45 p.m. people are beginning to follow us around the town, asking us questions. Mademoiselle de le Branchardière would have been proud to see her semicircular veil photographed in front of the old Wool Hall where fleeces had been sold years ago. Ice-creams all around, then up the hill towards the Guildhall, where Alexis spots a delightful orange-red cottage—it is just the spot for the Cherry Leaf shawl. Maria sits on the steps, looking as though she lives there."

Jane's, and your, Victorian adventure continues, for 14 glorious, consecutive days of sunshine. Before leaving, there's one more adventure to go: you treat yourself—and the XRX photo crew—to a ride on the London Eye, the popular ferris wheel that towers above the English capital.

London's panorama spreads at your feet. There are the Houses of Parliament; Hyde Park; Kensington Palace, Queen Victoria's birthplace; and the Queen Victoria Memorial in front of Buckingham Palace. England's longest reigning monarch holds the orb and scepter, but from high above, the latter looks a lot like a knitting needle.—*Alexis Xenakis, Sioux Falls, South Dakota*

(Clockwise, from bottom left) A new photo assistant; lace prepping; clocks dot the horizon: London's Big Ben, 1679 Cambridge dial, Belton House clock tower; Jane serves lunch; feasting on the steps of Belton House; Jane's veggie and cheese snacks, dahlia petals on the side; lunch board; Alexis and Mike stand guard; remember, look to the right before crossing; phone home; wrong platform—we're going to Cambridge, not Hogwarts!

195